Journeys with God

Marilyn D. Harris

Journeys with God
Marilyn D. Harris, MSN, RN, NEA-BC, FAAN
1 Shepherd's Way - Suite 207
Warminster, PA 18974
215-672-9773 • mharris555@verizon.net

Table of Contents

Table of Contents 2
Introduction 6
About the Author 8
Dedication 8
Acknowledgements 9
Scripture References 9
Part I – Devotions 11
Journeys to Far Away Places 11
    Journey to England – Give of Yourself 13
    Journey to Switzerland – Restoration 14
    Journey to Vienna – Please Touch 15
    Journey to the Soviet Union (1) – Precious Freedom 16
    Journey to the Soviet Union (2) – Liberty and Justice for All ... 17
    Journey to China – Fear of the Unknown 18
    Journey to San Francisco – Source of Power 20
    Journey to Bermuda – Daily Diligence 21
    Journey to Holland – Give Thanks in All Circumstances 22
    Journey by Air – Destination Confirmed 24
    Journey on an Ocean Liner (1) – Our Eternal Pilot 25
    Journey on an Ocean Liner (2) – Sound the Alarm 26
    Journey on an Ocean Liner (3) – Clean Hands – Pure Heart .. 27
    Journey to the City (1) – Useless Treasures 28
    Journey to the City (2) – Temperature Rising 29
    Journey on the Highway – A Good Samaritan 30

Journey Down the River – Spiritual Buoyancy 31
Journey to Visit Family – A Child is Born 32
Journey Abroad – Our Power Source 33
Journey on the Turnpike – Wait on the Lord 34
Journey to a Hotel – The Debt is Paid 35

Journeys Around Town 37
Journey to a Restaurant – Charge My Account 39
Journey to the Drug Store – Multiple Blessings 40
Journey to a Concert (1) – A Joyful Symphony 41
Journey to a Concert (2) – Unheralded Performance 42
Journey to the Grocery Store (1) – One Small Task 43
Journey to the Grocery Store (2) – Unexpected Sight 44
Journey to a Friend – Temporary Residence 45
Journey to the Office – Instant Communications 46
Journey to Church (1) – Faith at Work 47
Journey to Church (2) – Substantial Evidence 48
Journey to Church (3) – The Page Turner 49
Journey to a Seminar – Bumper Stickers 50
Journey to the Parking Lot – Hidden Danger 51
Journey to a Small Town Christmas – What Will We Give Him? 52
Journey up the Street – Beautiful Inside 53
Journey on the Train – One Track Line 54
Journey to the Department Store – Unique Characteristics 55
Journey to Somewhere – God's Plan 56
Journey to the City – Riding Backwards 57
Journey as an Administrator – Yielding Daily to God 58
Journey to Hatboro – Making a Difference 59

Journeys Around the House 61
    Journey to the Back Porch – Hidden Beauty 63
    Journey to the Kitchen (1) – Positive Outcomes 64
    Journey to the Kitchen (2) – Spiritual Nutrition 65
    Journey to the Front Yard – New Growth 67
    Journey to the Garden (1) – Room to Grow 68
    Journey to the Garden (2) – Vital Nourishment 69
    Journey to the Side Porch – A Child's Curiosity 70
    Journey to the Front Porch – The Victor 71
    Journey to the Basement – God's Power 72
    Journey Down the Lane – Guiding Light 73
    Journey to the Porch – Sparrows are Important 74
    Journey to Wholeness – A Clean Heart 75
    Journey with Kindness – Gracious Words 76
    Journey Through the Mail – God's Free Gift 77
    Journey to Court – Subject to a Higher Power 78

Journeys with Family and Friends 79
    Journey with Grief – A Special Prayer 81
    Journey with Memories – A Tribute to Mother 82
    Journey on a Sailplane – Total Dependence on God 83
    Journey for a New Car – Wrong Assumptions 84
    Journey on a Bicycle – Switching Gears 85
    Journey in the Dark – Let Your Light Shine 86
    Journey with a Child – God's Wireless Connection 87
    Journey Through Searching – One Lost Coin 88
    Journey for Clothes – At All Times 89
    Journey to the Hospital – A New Heart 90

- Journey with New Birth – A Child is Born 91
- Journey as a Caregiver – Multiple Challenges 92

Journeys by Those with Physical Challenges 95
- Journey to a Doctor's Office – Honest Words 97
- Journey to a Hospital (1) – Coronary Care 98
- Journey to a Hospital (2) – Trauma Alert 99
- Journey with Blindness – Walk by Faith 100
- Journey with Arthritis – Helping Hands 101
- Journey with Disability – Sturdy Vessels 102
- Journey with Grief – Do it Now! 103
- Journey after Surgery – Silent Partner 104
- Journey with Terminal Illness – Seasons of Life 105
- Journey with Facts – Beauty is Skin Deep 106
- Journey with Weights – To be Free 107

Part II – Reflections 109
- Childhood Memories 111
- The Patchwork Quilt 113
- The View from the Other Side of the Bed 116
- Up, Up and Away! 118
- One Special Family 120
- "Hello, I Think I Know You." 122
- Qualities – Past and Present 124
- My Fondest Memories of Nursing 127
- You Tell on Yourself 132
- Journeys Through All Seasons of Life 133

Introduction

The Old and New Testaments describe the journeys experienced by many individuals. The children of Israel experienced many challenges on their way to the Promised Land. God was with them on their journey. Exodus: 40:36-38. The men on the road to Emmaus met the risen Christ. They said to each other, "Did not our hearts burn within us while he talked to us on the road, while he opened to us the scriptures?" Luke 24:32. This scripture reference has a special meaning for me since I was born and lived in Emmaus, Pennsylvania for the first 18 years of life. It was during these years when I attended Bethel Bible Fellowship Church in Emmaus, Pennsylvania that I met the risen Christ during a Saturday morning Bible club meeting.

Everyday each of us begins a journey. Sometimes our experiences keep us in our homes, backyards, communities, workplaces or take us to faraway places. Our experiences provide as many challenges and are as varied as the individuals we meet. Whatever the circumstances, we are not alone, God is with us.

The Merriam-Webster.com dictionary describes a journey as the act of traveling from one place to another. Our journeys are not always smooth and they do not always follow our plan. I usually drive the same familiar route from my home to Center City Philadelphia, Pennsylvania. One day road construction made it necessary for me to detour through an unfamiliar neighborhood. It was a pleasant surprise to see the beautiful homes and flowers just off the busy roadway.

There are many times when we, and those around us, experience detours in life: chronic or acute illness, accidents, disappointments, unfulfilled dreams and/or death. At that moment, these detours are very real, sometimes painful or, at least, an inconvenience. But later, like my traffic detour, they often reveal wonderful and unexpected results. It is during some of life's detours that we have the opportunity to slow down, reflect on goals, count our blessings and rely on God's wisdom for the unknown future. What we may consider a detour is part of God's plan for each of us.

My first 80 years have been a wonderful journey with God. *Journeys with God* consists of two parts. Part I includes devotions. Some of the devotions in Part One were written and published beginning in 1985 by Judson Press, Valley Forge, Pennsylvania. Recent devotions are online at www.livingseasonsministry.com.

Part II includes reflection based on articles I wrote to share my personal and professional nursing experiences over the past 60 years. Five articles were published in *Vital Woman* (American Baptist Women's Ministries) in 2006 and 2007 and are used with permission. Additional reflections are from my "memory books" that include thoughts and photographs during my lifetime. I share them with you with gratitude to God for his faithfulness during all of my journeys during my first 80 years.

About the Author

Marilyn D. Harris, MSN, RN, NEA-BC, FAAN received her diploma from Abington Memorial Hospital School of Nursing and her baccalaureate and master's degrees (MSN) in nursing from the University of Pennsylvania School of Nursing. She was a staff nurse, supervisor, and the executive director of Abington Hospital Home Care and Hospice for 22 years prior to her retirement in 1999. She is a nurse executive advanced- board certified (NEA-BC) and was inducted as a Fellow in the American Academy of Nursing (FAAN) in 1988.

Marilyn is a member of Hatboro Baptist Church, Hatboro, PA, where she is an elder, Sunday school teacher and a faith community nurse. In addition to her faith-based devotions and articles, Marilyn has published many professional articles and several books.

Dedication

This book is dedicated to the memory of my husband, Charlie, who died on September 12, 2014. He loved, supported, and encouraged me during our 45 years of marriage and throughout my nursing career.

Acknowledgements

Thank you to Alan Russell for assisting me to develop my idea to collect my personal writings and put them into one book to share with my family and friends. I appreciate his editorial and production skills. I was introduced to Alan, who attends Bethel Bible Fellowship Church in Emmaus, Pennsylvania, by one of my cousins. I found out during one of my early conversations with Alan that he knew my mother (Florence Dickert) for several years before her death in 1988. They both attended Bethel Bible Fellowship Church in Emmaus, Pennsylvania.

Several devotions were originally published in *Women at the Well: Meditations on Healing and Wholeness* edited by Mary L. Mild, Copyright 1996 and *Women at the Well, Volume 2: Meditations for Quenching our Thirst* edited by Linda-Marie Delloff and Bernadette Glover Williams, Copyright 2003 by Judson Press. Used by permission.

Scripture References

All of the scripture references are from the New Revised International Version of the Bible unless noted that they are from The Entire Living Bible (TLB).

Part I – Devotions

Journeys to Far Away Places

Journey to England – Give of Yourself

Psalm 19:7. *The law of the Lord is perfect reviving the soul.*

"Please talk to me, I'm lonely." This was the inscription on the badge worn by one young man standing on a milk crate at Speaker's Corner in Hyde Park in London, England. Through conversation my husband and I determined that this young man did not want friends; he just wanted to talk. "I never smile," he said, "because a smile is the beginning of friendship. A smile leads to an exchange of names and this requires that I give something of myself away and I'm not willing to do that."

Many people we meet each day do not express their feelings as openly as did this young man, yet there are many lonely people among our daily contacts. Why not share a smile and conversation with them and give something of yourself away?

Prayer: Let the words of my mouth and meditation of my heart be acceptable to you, O Lord, my rock and my redeemer. (Psalm 19:14). Amen.

Journey to Switzerland – Restoration

Psalm 121:1. *I will lift up my eyes to the hill – from where will my help come?*

The Swiss Alps were beautiful to visit. There were the snow covered mountain tops, the green fields, and the delicate flowers. One morning after a heavy rain, the mountains appeared the same but the grass and flowers were laid low with moisture. After a few hours the sun came out and the flowers began to spring back to life. They had been bruised but not destroyed.

There are experiences in our lives that affect us like the rain affected the flowers. We feel beaten down by failures, disappointments, circumstances, and responsibilities. But, our strength to bounce back to life comes from the source of eternal life. It is God who restores our soul on a regular basis and enables us to carry on with life and enjoy our blessings.

Prayer: Thank you for the refreshing rains that help to beautify our surroundings and the lessons they teach us about you. Amen.

Journey to Vienna – Please Touch

Psalm 100:3. *Know that the Lord is God. It is he that made us, and we are his.*

On a music tour of Vienna, Austria, I visited the home of Franz Lehar. Accustomed to the usual "Do Not Touch" signs that one usually finds in museums, I was surprised when the caretaker brought out a book of Lehar's compositions and invited anyone who wished to do so to play the composer's piano. I accepted this once in a lifetime offer that I shall remember for many years.

Our Heavenly Father has created many masterpieces. These, like Lehar's piano, are to be enjoyed and experienced instead of looked at from a distance. Snowcapped mountain peaks, delicate flowers, a beautiful sunset, and many other daily experiences remind us that our Lord is God. He has created us as well as the beauty all around us.

Prayer: Father, thank you for the many reminders of your creation in our daily life. In Jesus' name, Amen

Marilyn playing Franz Lehar's Piano

Journey to the Soviet Union (1) – Precious Freedom

John 8:36. *So if the Son makes you free, you will be free indeed.*

During a public health study tour of the Soviet Union our Intourist guide developed a blister on her heel while taking us on a walking tour of the Kremlin. One of the nurses in our group had a band aid. Our guide sat on a low wall while a nurse offered first aid. Several other nurses huddled around to watch the action. Within seconds, a soldier moved us back so that he could determine what was happening in the circle. After a few words with our guide, the soldier smiled and left. It was both enlightening and frightening to note that even a small, innocent gathering did not go unnoticed.

Freedom to gather in public places, attend church, pray, work, shop for food in abundance – these are just a few of my many blessings to thank God for on a daily basis.

Prayer: Father, thank you for uncounted blessings. We pray for fellow Christians who cannot enjoy these same freedoms. Amen.

Journey to the Soviet Union (2) – Liberty and Justice for All

John 8:36. *So if the Son makes you free, you will be free indeed.*

I was on a public health nurse study tour in the former Soviet Union when the words "with liberty and justice for all" from the Pledge of Allegiance to the United States flag flashed through my mind. During my professional visit I was not free from rules or restrictions. Although I was able to shop, walk in town, go to church, ride the subway or take a taxi, there were certain circumstances that made me aware that I was not free. The militia and soldiers were everywhere- on the streets, in doorways, cars, and restaurants, blowing whistles if I moved outside the white lines, using a sound system from their automobiles or from towers on the highway.

Each time I registered in a hotel I had to surrender my passport and visa until I checked out of the hotel. I was not going very far without these credentials! In each hotel a floor lady was on duty twenty-four hours a day. The hotel room keys were under her control. I presented my guest card to her, and she gave me the key to my room. I returned the key to her when I left my room for the day. I felt as if my every move was monitored. I did not feel free although I was not confined to a specific place.

Prayer: Dear Lord, every day Christian women around the world experience the constraints that I felt for a few weeks. Thank you for the spiritual freedom that is ours through your Son, regardless of our physical circumstances. Amen.

Reprinted from *Women at the Well: Meditations for Quenching Our Thirst. Volume 2* edited by Linda-Marie Delloff and Bernadette Glover-Williams, copyright © 2003 by Judson Press. Used by permission of Judson Press.

Journey to China – Fear of the Unknown

Joshua 1:9. *I hereby command you: Be strong and courageous; do not be frightened or dismayed, for the Lord your God is with you wherever you go.*

Several years ago, and a short time after the student protests, I visited Beijing, China as a member of a People to People tour for public health nurses. In addition to our professional visits to hospitals, clinics, and homes, we enjoyed sightseeing. One stop was on Tiananmen Square. Our local guide shared information on several point of interest and then encouraged us (forty nurses) to explore the square on our own in small groups for about thirty minutes. Prior to leaving us on our own, our guide gave us directions to find our bus by using our last site as a point of reference.

After a few minutes of walking around the area, there was increased security activity on the square. Several busloads of soldiers arrive in front of one building. The soldiers stood shoulder-to-shoulder and began to march across the square, clearing it of all visitors. Everyone had to move in a direction away from where we were to meet the bus and our guide. Our small group looked for familiar faces of other tour members in the crowd. We finally spotted a few friendly faces. Our hearts and pulses were pounding since no one could tell us what had happened to initiate this clearing of the square. Eventually, all of the tour members found their way to our bus. Our local guide learned that the square was cleared merely to prepare the area for the arrival of a visiting dignitary.

This experience with the unknown is probably the most frightening experience I have ever had in a foreign country. It was very disconcerting to be denied freedom of movement without knowing what was happening or why.

Christian women in many countries experience this kind of fear and oppression daily. Their movement is restricted, as are their outward expressions of faith. My own experience of fear, even in what was a relatively safe setting, has increased my awareness of the uncertainty that many women live with throughout their lives.

Prayer: Dear Lord, thank you for the freedom that I enjoy in America. I pray in Jesus' name for Christian women throughout the world who do not have this privilege. Amen.

Reprinted from Women at the Well, Volume 2: Meditations for Quenching Our Thirst edited by Linda-Marie Delloff and Bernadette Glover-Williams, copyright @ 2003 by Judson Press. Used by permission of Judson Press.

Eating with chopsticks in China

Journey to San Francisco – Source of Power

Psalm 21:13. *Accept our praise, O Lord, for all your glorious power (TLB).*

The cable cars of San Francisco are fascinating to a first time visitor. These cars are able to manage steep hills and sharp declines through the use of power that is hidden from sight. The power is generated from a central source that is made available to the individual cars through underground cables.

Christians also have an almighty power source that is able to provide the strength necessary to meet the ups and downs experienced in our daily lives. Our central power, though unseen, is evident in how we are able to meet the challenges of each day through our faith and trust in God.

Prayer: Dear Father, thank you for guiding us each day through your power. In Jesus' name, Amen.

Journey to Bermuda – Daily Diligence

Psalm 118:24. *This is the day that the Lord hath made; let us rejoice and be glad in it.*

During a recent vacation my room overlooked the hotel's swimming pool. Each morning the hotel staff cleaned the patio and arranged the lounge chairs in rows around the pool. Each afternoon when I returned to the room and looked out of my window the chairs were facing many directions and strewn with towels. This same pattern repeated itself for five days.

These chairs are so typical of many days. I start with everything in order, devotions, lists of things to be done, goals to meet. But, by the end of the day, everything is topsy-turvy for various reasons. Like the hotel staff, I need to be diligent in my responsibilities and accept the activities that rearrange my best laid plans on specific days. Each day is a day to rejoice.

Prayer: Dear God, I am thankful for each day that you give me to serve you and to enjoy the world that you created. Amen.

Journey to Holland – Give Thanks in All Circumstances

I Thessalonians 5:12-18. *But we appeal to you, brothers and sisters, to respect those who labor among you, and have charge of you in the Lord and admonish you; esteem them very highly in love because of their work. Be at peace among yourselves. And we urge you, beloved, to admonish the idlers, encourage the faint hearted, help the weak, be patient with all of them. See that none of you repays evil for evil, but always seek to do good to one another and to all. Rejoice always, pray without ceasing, give thanks in all circumstances; for this is the will of God in Christ Jesus for you.*

Years ago, I read *The Hiding Place* written by Corrie ten Boom (1971). She described the life that she and her family experienced in Haarlem, Holland, before and during the German occupation during World War II, and later in concentration camps. The family's home was a hiding place for Jewish neighbors and friends. The back jacket of the book includes a schematic drawing of the house. Corrie describes a false wall that was built in one of the bedrooms that concealed a small cramped area where people could hide for safety and items could be stored on short notice.

In 1988, I had the opportunity to visit Haarlem and walk along the Barteljorisstraat (street) where Corrie's home and store are located. Although I could not enter, thanks to the schematic drawing of the house, I was able to visualize the activity that took place in this small home prior to and during WW II.

Throughout the book, Corrie shares the determinations and courage that she and her family exhibited following their arrest for concealing Jews during the Nazi occupation and as the family members lived and died in the concentration camps prior to Corrie's liberation in 1945.

Corrie and her family stilled themselves to know God better, regardless of their circumstances. The family stilled themselves each morning and night prior to the war for Bible reading and prayer. Scripture reading was at 8:30 AM each morning for all who were in the house. This was one fixed point around which life revolved. This same scene is repeated night after night when she and her family had few possessions, saw their neighbors and friends taken into captivity, not knowing when they would be next.

After the family's arrest, a group gathered around Corrie's father for prayer each evening. They no longer had a Bible but much of God's word was stored in their hearts. Their devotional time continued in the concentration camps whether in solitary confinement or in the larger barracks. What wonderful examples of disciples who worshipped God regardless of their circumstances.

Prayer: Dear Father, our prayers are for the many women and men around the world who experience less than ideal, and many times, dangerous circumstances every day of their lives. Thank you for the relative safety I experience each day and for your loving care in all of my circumstances. In Jesus' name. Amen.

Reference: ten Boom, C. (1971). *The Hiding Place*. Chosen Books. Washington Depot, CT.

Reprinted with permission from an online devotion for American Baptist Women's Ministry. October 31, 2006.

Journey by Air – Destination Confirmed

Matthew 5:16. *Let your light shine before others so that they may see your good works and give glory to your Father in heaven.*

I was on a flight from the east coast to the mid-west to attend a business meeting. As the plane neared its destination I pulled a program brochure from my briefcase to review the local transportation options to my hotel. A fellow passenger, seated behind me, introduced herself and asked if we could share a ride to the hotel. She had recognized the brochure I was reading and identified me as someone who was headed for the same meeting she planned to attend.

Through non-verbal communication I had told a fellow passenger something about my professional association and my destination. Do I convey this same type of non-verbal communication about the spiritual aspects of my life to those who observe my activities each day?

Prayer: Dear Father, help me to be a good example to others and show them the way to our heavenly destination. Amen.

Journey on an Ocean Liner (1) – Our Eternal Pilot

Mark 4:40. *Why are you afraid? Have you still no faith?*

The words of the hymn "*Jesus, Savior, Pilot Me*" came to mind when I took my first cruise. The ship had a captain and crew who were qualified to see the ship safely through an unmarked ocean. But, this was not enough. The ship needed a pilot who was familiar with local waters to take the ship safely in and out of port. The captain welcomed the pilot on board.

At times, we feel that we are the captain and very much in control. Although we are well-prepared, experienced, responsible, and (possibly) charged with the safety of those around us, we, like the ship's captain, must relinquish the controls. We must trust in Jesus Christ, our Savior and Pilot, who knows the unseen dangers, shallow waters, and the unmarked course to our eternal home.

Prayer: Dear Father, thank you for being acquainted with all our ways. Guide us in all we do. In Jesus' name, Amen.

Journey on an Ocean Liner (2) – Sound the Alarm

I Thessalonians 5:18. *Rejoice always, pray without ceasing, and give thanks in all circumstances for this is the will of God in Christ Jesus for you.*

The sound of seven short and one long bell and alarms on a ship signals an emergency. At the start of a cruise there is no anxiety during the mandatory safety drill. The response is much different when the bells and alarms sound at night while at sea.

The announcer over the loudspeaker said: "A fire has been detected. All crew report to assigned fire stations, medical personnel report to the infirmary, all guests on a specific deck go to your emergency muster station. All other guests remain in your cabins until further notice."

My husband, I, and fellow passengers in our immediate area were outside our cabins and on high alert while we waited for the next announcement. It was impossible to relax, not knowing exactly what was happening on another part of the ship. About one hour later, the captain advised everyone that the fire was extinguished, everyone was safe, and displaced passengers could return to their cabins. I knew the emergency procedure but the thought of actually having to evacuate the ship in the dark of night was much different from the practice earlier in the cruise.

Prayer: Father, some of life's experiences can be anticipated and planned for but there is no comparison to the actual events. Thank you that you are our refuge and strength, a very present help in trouble (Psalm 46:1). Amen.

Journey on an Ocean Liner (3) – Clean Hands – Pure Heart

Psalm 24:4-5. *He that has clean hands and a pure heart…shall receive the blessing from the Lord and righteousness from the God of his salvation.*

On a recent cruise everyone was instructed to wash their hands on a frequent basis. The goal was to keep guests healthy and free from infections that could spread to other guests. In addition to written instructions and automatic dispensers of hand-washing gel, cruise staff was positioned at the entrance to all of the dining areas. The words "Washy-Washy" accompanied the manual dispensing of gel as we entered the dining areas.

From observation, most guests had clean hands. But, what about a pure heart? Scripture reminds us that man looks on the outward appearance but God looks on the heart. Only God knows if our heart is pure.

Prayer: Father, thank you for dying for my sins and for creating in me a clean heart through believing in you. Amen.

Journey to the City (1) – Useless Treasures

Matthew 6:20. *...but, store up for yourselves treasures in heaven…*

On a recent train ride to the city a mother and her three children sat nearby. One of the boys, about three years old, walked through the car and picked up the ticket stubs that previous passengers had discarded. He held them tightly in his hand and would not share them with anyone.

During the one-hour ride he became tired and lay down on an empty seat across the aisle from me. He held onto his stubs with a tight fist, but as he dozed off to sleep, his grip relaxed and the useless stubs scattered to the floor.

At times, each one of us holds onto useless things that seem very important at a given time. It is more important to lay up treasures in heaven than hold onto material things that are worthless when compared with God's gifts to us.

Prayer: Father, help us to evaluate our priorities and let go of those things that are worthless in your sight. Amen.

Journey to the City (2) – Temperature Rising

Proverbs 3:21. *Have these two goals, wisdom, that is knowing and doing right and common sense.* (TLB).

It was 6:30 AM as I rode the local train to the city to keep an early appointment. The temperature was already 75 degrees and humid. The train made an unscheduled stop between stations. The conductor announced that a switch was frozen. "That's right folks. The switch is frozen. Needed work is being done to correct the problem. Sit back and relax."

There are times when I freeze or don't function as planned when emotional temperatures get hot. Too many things to do or unexpected interruptions cause reactions that are not typical responses to a specific situation A practical solution to master these day-to-day situations at home and at work is for me to stop, evaluate, relax and try to correct the problem rather than contributing to it.

Prayer: Dear Father, teach me to seek your wisdom in dealing with all of the unexpected as well as planned experiences each day. Amen.

Journey on the Highway – A Good Samaritan

Luke 10:29, 37. *…And who is my neighbor?... The one who showed him mercy. Jesus said to him: "Go and do likewise."*

A friend of mine and several other drivers experienced flat tires when they hit a boulder that suddenly appeared on a busy interstate highway. All of the drivers pulled to the side of the road to assess their damages.

One of the other drivers indicated he would help my friend as soon as he changed his own tire and helped those around him. When my friend's turn came for help, the stranger changed her tire, led the way to a service station where she could buy a tire, shared a snack with her at a fast food restaurant while the tire was changed and prayed with her before she continued her interrupted journey home. This individual interrupted his schedule for four hours to help strangers of different sexes, races and ages. He was a modern day Good Samaritan.

Prayer: In today's world we are often afraid to befriend strangers. Help us to follow the example you set for us. In Jesus' name, Amen.

Journey Down the River – Spiritual Buoyancy

Psalm 119:117. *Hold me up that I may be safe….*

My husband and I spend our summers along a river where the favorite sport is "tubing down the river". Individuals come from miles around to wade into the river and sit or hold onto any floatation device such as an inner tube and allow the river to carry them downstream to a specific destination. This is a delightful way to spend an afternoon; floating on top of the calm water or riding the waves created by passing boats. One important aspect of this experience is to place one's faith on the unseen air that inflates the tube.

As Christians, we are filled with the Holy Spirit. This spiritual buoyancy enables us to stay afloat. During periods of calm or stress we are upheld by God's hand and we are safe because of our faith in Jesus Christ, God's Son.

Prayer: Dear God, thank you for filling us with your Holy Spirit. In Jesus' name, Amen

Journey to Visit Family – A Child is Born

Luke 2:11. *To you is born this day in the city of David, a Savior who is the Messiah, the Lord.*

During the past year three of my friends became grandparents for the first time. Each new grandson and his parents lived hundreds of miles from where the grandparents lived. During the Christmas holiday each family headed for different parts of the United States to adore a newborn child.

As I shared with my friends in their joy at the birth of their special grandchildren I also remembered the shepherds and wise men who traveled many miles to worship and adore a newborn baby almost 2000 years ago.

During this Christmas season let us, like the shepherds, sing praises to God for sending his Son to us and for all we have heard and seen.

Prayer: Dear Father, thank you for the birth of your Son, Jesus Christ. Help us to worship and adore you each day. Amen.

Journey Abroad – Our Power Source

Luke 24:49…I am sending upon you what my Father promised; so stay here in the city until you have been clothed with power from on high.

When traveling in countries that have direct rather than alternating current for electricity I need to take an electric converter as well as an adapter to use an electrical appliance. The adapter makes it possible to fit the appliance into the power source. But, the converter is required to make the power change possible. If the adapter is used without the converter, the appliance will burn out – as I discovered!

This is a practical explanation of how Jesus Christ is our power source. He told us that no man cometh to the Father but through Him. Our salvation is not by our works but through the death and resurrection of our Lord. It is not adequate that we adapt – we need to be converted through the power of Jesus who died for our sins.

Prayer: Dear Father, thank you for providing eternal life through Jesus Christ to everyone who believes that you died for their sins. Thank you that you are our power source from on high. In Jesus' name, Amen.

Journey on the Turnpike – Wait on the Lord

Psalm 130:5. *I wait for the Lord, my soul waits, and in his word I put my hope.*

I met a fellow traveler at an interstate rest stop who look puzzled as she searched for a way to turn on the water faucet to wash her hands. I was familiar with the automatic sensor type faucet and I suggested she simply place her hands under the faucet and the water would begin to flow – and it did.

There are many times when I spend time looking for ways to solve perceived problems or change situations. God has made provision to meet my needs. I must place myself in God's hands each day and wait to receive His blessings that flow freely.

Prayer: Give us patience to wait and thankful hearts that praise you for blessings that we enjoy each day. In Jesus' name, Amen.

Journey to a Hotel – The Debt is Paid

Luke 10:35. *Take care of him; and when I come back, I will repay you whatever more you spend.*

When I travel on business I register at the hotel, sign my name, and agree to pay a specific dollar amount per night. At times, when I check out, the bill reflects a zero balance since the bill has been charged to a master account for my employer and has been paid in full. This occurs because someone else assumed the debt associated with my stay.

Jesus Christ paid the price for my salvation by dying on the cross for my sins. He took on himself my sins. I am forgiven, my debt is paid, by believing on Jesus Christ as my Lord and savior.

Prayer: Dear Father, thank you for the forgiveness of sins for everyone who believes that you died and rose again so that we may have everlasting life. In Jesus' name, Amen.

Journeys Around Town

Journey to a Restaurant – Charge My Account

Luke 10:35. *Take care of him and when I come back I will repay you whatever more you spend.*

My husband and I were celebrating my birthday at a local restaurant known for its excellent food and service. We were already eating when several other people were seated next to us. One of the arriving guests accidently bumped our table while being seated and knocked over the filled glasses, spilling the contents onto the table, my skirt, and jacket.

The manager saw what happened and immediately came to our table. After helping to soak up the liquids, he offered me his card with instructions to send him the cleaning bill. Although he had not contributed to the incident, he assumed responsibility for the results.

Jesus offered to take responsibility for our sins, although he was sinless, so that those who believe may have eternal life.

Prayer: Father, thank you for dying on the cross for my sins so that I may have life everlasting. Amen.

Journey to the Drug Store – Multiple Blessings

Psalm 92:1. *It is good to give thanks to the Lord….*

I grew up in a small town. My family celebrated special occasions by going to a drug store in town that had a soda fountain. The individual who was celebrating a special occasion such as a birthday or good report card was allowed to ask for one extra cherry on top of an ice cream sundae for each special event. Life then was simple.

Today, life is more complex. However, I often enjoy the fond memories of those family celebrations. Many times, as I name my blessings, I think of the many cherries I would have on my sundae if I could relive those childhood experiences.

How many cherries would you have on your imaginary sundae if you added one for each of God's blessings during the past days and weeks?

Prayer: Now glory be to God who…is able to do far more than we would ever dare to ask or even dream… (Ephesians 3:20). (TLB). Amen.

Journey to a Concert (1) – A Joyful Symphony

Psalm 98:6. *Let the cornets and trumpets shout! Make a joyful symphony before the Lord, the King!* (TLB)

Prior to a concert, each orchestra member tunes up his or her instrument and practices scales. The sound that results is one of noise and confusion. But when the concert master appears, all the members tune their instruments to one note. The sound that we hear when the conductor begins the concert is one of musical pleasure.

Our lives and surrounds often resemble the orchestra prior to the conductor's appearance; a cacophony of untuned lives. We need someone to bring order and harmony to our lives. Jesus Christ, our Lord and Savior, is available to lead us and conduct our lives in ways that will bring praise to him.

Prayer: O Lord, help us to make a joyful noise to you because of the marvelous things you have done for us. Amen.

Journey to a Concert (2) – Unheralded Performance

Matthew 6:4. *Your Father who sees in secret will reward you.*

I attended a piano concert. The pianist's talents were enhanced by the support of a full concert orchestra. This unheralded group, situated in the orchestra pit, mostly out of sight, provided valuable support to the featured artist. Although their individual contributions were not heralded, they were very important to the overall success of the performance.

This same concept applies in many of life's situation. Behind the featured speaker, artist, and newscaster are many people who contribute to a successful program. Examples in our local church are those individuals who are responsible for ordering and delivering the altar flowers, lighting the candles, turning up the heat, arranging for child care, sharpening the pew pencils and preparing communion for the benefit of others.

Prayer: Help us to be thankful for the many people who are responsible for the little things in our everyday life. Amen.

Journey to the Grocery Store (1) – One Small Task

Ecclesiastes 3:14. *I know that whatsoever God does endures forever.*

Our local grocery store recently installed new scanner registers that read manufacturers' codes. While waiting in line to pay my bill I became aware that this particular register wasn't functioning properly. The cashier had to put the same item over the scanner several times. Frequently, she had to manually input the price.

I commented: "I notice that your new register isn't working properly." Her reply was: "It's my fault. The glass is dirty. I should take the time to clean it."

I was reminded that many times things have to be done over and over again. How many times should I have taken the time to do that one small task that would have made life much easier and more pleasant for me and those around me?

Prayer: Dear God, Help us to use each opportunity to do one small deed for you. In Jesus' name, Amen.

Journey to the Grocery Store (2) – Unexpected Sight

I Samuel 16:7. *For the Lord does not see as mortals see; they look on the outward appearance, but the Lord looks on the heart.*

I stopped at the local grocery store late one evening and met a professional acquaintance who had also stopped at the store on her way home from swimming. She greeted me with: "I was hoping that I wouldn't meet anyone I know since I look terrible." She was referring to her appearance that included wet hair and a swim suit cover-up rather than her usual well-kept appearance that I am accustomed to seeing in our professional relationship.

Most of the time each of us tries to look his or her best for friends and business associates. Our scripture for today reminds us that although this appearance is important to us, God is concerned with our relations with Him and how this is conveyed to those people with whom we have contact each day.

Prayer: Father, help each of us to remember those aspects of life that are important to you as well as to our friends. Amen.

Journey to a Friend – Temporary Residence

Psalm 118:24. *This is the day that the Lord has made; let us rejoice and be glad in it.*

The husband of one of my friends is an architect. He designed and built their contemporary home. I prefer colonial structures. Our conversations frequently center around architecture.

My friend's young son, Steve, who was just learning to talk, was in the room one evening when we became involved in yet another discussion. Steve chimed in: "I live in a temporary house." He had tried to describe the design of his house and, without knowing it, had spoken a spiritual truth.

Our bodies are temporary houses. Each day and each blessing is a gift from God. Let us use every opportunity to serve God during our journey to our eternal home.

Prayer: Dear Father, thank you for Jesus Christ, the rock of our salvation and strong foundation. In Jesus' name, Amen.

Journey to the Office – Instant Communications

I Samuel 3:10. *And Samuel said: Speak, for your servant is listening.*

During the work day in the 1980s I had access to two types of office machines that made it possible to communicate across miles by means of telephone lines. One of these was a computer with a modem; the other was a telephone facsimile machine. A message, information, or drawing in one office could be reproduced at another site in a very short period of time. Although I do not understand all of the details of technology that make this possible, I know that both the sender and receiver have to be in a "ready" mode for this process to occur.

The Lord says: "Call to me and I will answer you, and will tell you great and hidden things that you have not known." May we respond like Samuel: "Speak, Lord, for your servant is listening."

Prayer: Dear Father, you are always ready to hear us when we speak to you. Help us to listen and respond to your answers. In Jesus' name, Amen.

Journey to Church (1) – Faith at Work

Hebrews 11:1. *Now faith is the assurance of things hoped for, the conviction of things not seen.*

The teacher told the class that he had a quarter in his coat pocket. He invited anyone who believed what he was saying to come forward and take the coin from his pocket and keep it. I remember being very interested in his offer since the quarter represented my weekly allowance at that time. While I was daydreaming about what I could do with the twenty-five cents one of the other children went forward to claim his reward – sight unseen!

The teacher then told us that we could place our faith in Jesus Christ like one of the children had placed his faith in the words of the teacher. That day, approximately 70 years ago, I placed my faith in Jesus Christ and have been trusting Him ever since to meet my needs.

Prayer: Throughout the years faith has sustained those who believe in you. Thank you for your faithfulness to us. Amen.

Journey to Church (2) – Substantial Evidence

Matthew 5:16. *Let your light shine before others, so that they may see your good work and give glory to your Father in heaven.*

The question on the bulletin board in front of a local church asked: "If you were arrested for being a Christian, would there be enough evidence to convict you?"

I thought of the evidence that could be presented at my hearing or trial. My immediate family could report that I read the Bible, pray, and write meditations. My neighbors could confirm that I attend worship on Sunday. A wider public could testify that they read meditations of mine that have been published.

But, would there be any surprise evidence such as how I reacted under pressure at work, or when I thought no one else saw me? I am thankful that there is still time and opportunity to accumulate additional evidence that can be used in support of my Christian faith.

Prayer: Father, help each of us to take advantage of every opportunity to share our faith with those we meet. Amen.

Journey to Church (3) – The Page Turner

Matthew 6:4 *….and your Father who sees in secret will reward you.*

I attended a special service at a church in our neighborhood. The pianist was playing before the service and I heard someone behind me say: "That's my granddaughter turning the pages." For the first time, I noticed a young girl seated on the bench next to the pianist. She was filling a very important role although she was unnoticed by most of the people, except her grandmother.

There are so many individuals who work behind the scene to help others succeed. Many times they serve without recognition, by choice, or because we fail to pay attention to what is happening around us.

Prayer: Father, there are many activities and distractions each day that we sometimes do not focus on what is important to you, others, and ourselves. Direct our hearts and minds to be attentive to your voice. In Jesus' name, Amen.

Journey to a Seminar – Bumper Stickers

Psalm 19:14. *Let the words of my mouth and the meditation of my heart be acceptable to you, O Lord, my rock and my redeemer.*

I attended a seminar where the speaker asked: "What kind of bumper sticker are you?" Everyone was given a few minutes to think about a response and write it down. Bumper stickers tell others where we have visited, what or who we support, and where we work plus much more. They are one method of silent communications. I had a hard time making a decision on the words that I wanted to display to the other attendees.

Fortunately, we did not have to share our answers at the seminar. But, I was reminded that there are multiple non-verbal bumper sticker messages that I convey to my family, friends, and co-workers each day. It is important that my silent messages be positive and convey my Christian faith.

Prayer: Dear Father, remind me that my actions speak louder than my words each day. In Jesus' name, Amen.

Journey to the Parking Lot – Hidden Danger

Psalm 38:12. *Those who seek my life set their snares, those who seek to hurt me speak of ruin and mediate treachery all day long.*

One spring day a mother duck took her ducklings for a walk on the parking lot that surrounds the office building where I worked. All went well until she walked over a water drainage ditch grate and her three ducklings fell to the bottom. It was the mother's noisy calls and her frenzied walk around the grate that alerted a passerby to her plight. The staff of the management corporation was able to remove the grate, lift the apparently unharmed ducklings to safety and stand by as the mother and her young family continue their interrupted walk to the safety of the nearby lawn.

There are countless hidden or unsuspecting actual and potential dangers and detours that are present in our daily activities. Although many of these may not be as dramatic as the ducks dilemma, each of us must be alert to the many circumstances that can impact us each day. We are dependent on God to lead and protect us each day.

Prayer: Dear Father, thank you that God is our refuge and strength, a very present help in trouble. (Psalm 46:1). In Jesus' name, Amen.

Journey to a Small Town Christmas – What Will We Give Him?

Isaiah 11:6...*and a little child shall lead them.*

Hatboro Baptist Church holds a Small Town Christmas for the community on a Saturday in December. This celebration includes music, crafts, skits, refreshments, and a live outdoor nativity with several petting animals. The nativity story is portrayed by adults and children at scheduled times. At the end of each live performance the children and adults are invited to take a closer look at the manger scene. One 3-year old child lingered at the manger where the baby Jesus lay (represented by a doll). Three times his mother attempted to move him away and three times the child returned to the manger. Before leaving the last time he placed the small candy cane he received at a previous activity in the manger. This spontaneous response by a 3-year old brought tears to the eyes of the participants as well as the audience. He gave what he had - his gift of a candy cane to Jesus. What will we give to Him this Christmas and throughout the year?

Prayer: Dear Father, you came to earth to give your life for each person who believes on you as their Lord and Savior. Remind us of your great love for us and the opportunity to share your love through our words and deeds every day. In Jesus' name, Amen.

Journey up the Street – Beautiful Inside

I Samuel 16.7....*for the Lord does not see as mortals see, they look on the outward appearance, but the Lord looks on the heart.*

The sign on the lawn read: "House for sale – beautiful inside." The exterior of the house was not the most appealing or inviting in the neighborhood. The owner, realizing this possible liability, extolled what was not apparent when potential buyers drive past the house.

This sale sign reminds me of the many people I know who are beautiful on the inside because of their Christian faith. Their beauty is evident in the many daily activities, unsung deeds and behind the scene involvement that are hidden from others.

Prayer: Dear Father, so much emphasis is placed on our physical appearance. Remind us that you look on our hearts. Amen.

Journey on the Train – One Track Line

Psalm 37:7a. *Be still before the Lord, and wait patiently for him.*

The trains to and from my home town into center city travel on one track. Since the north and southbound trains use the same track, at one point in the journey, one of the trains needs to wait on a siding just outside our town for a few minutes until the other train passes.

There are many examples when each of us, our family, or friends have to wait on the sideline while life seems to be passing by. Illness, disability, circumstances, or the death of a loved one impact our life. God has a purpose for each of us and our time is in His hands. He is in control when we are on the move or waiting on the sideline. Our challenge is to be still and know that He is God.

Prayer: Dear Father, in this fast paced world, it is hard for us to have patience. Remind us that you direct our journey through life and our times are in your hands. In Jesus' name, Amen.

Journey to the Department Store – Unique Characteristics

I Samuel 16:7. *But the Lord said to Samuel, "Do not look on his appearance or on the height of his stature, because I have rejected him; for the Lord does not see as mortals see; they look on the outward appearance, but the Lord looks on the heart."*

I bought a dress that included a tag that stated that "The gentle shading and slight irregularities and/or slubs which may appear on this garment are inherent to the natural fibers used in the manufacturing of the cloth and in no way reflect damage or errors in manufacturing." The tag's message reminds me of the diversity that contributes to our world today and that each of us is born with unique characteristics that develop and contribute beauty to our family, church, work, and community.

Prayer: Dear Father, help me to appreciate the uniqueness and experiences that each one brings to your world. Amen.

Journey to Somewhere – God's Plan

Jeremiah 29:11. *"For surely I know the plans I have for you, says the Lord, plans for your welfare and not for harm, to give you a future with hope."*

My husband and I take "mystery tours" with a local bus company. The only information we receive is the date(s) of the tour, plus the time and place to meet the bus. The events of the day(s) remain a mystery to everyone except the bus driver. On one of our recent tours we visited several museums, including one that offered a canal boat ride. On our last three-day tour, we stayed at a wonderful inn, had great meals, and saw new sights.

Today's scripture reminds me that God has plans for each day that he allows me to experience. Each morning I do not know what experiences, joys, or challenges will occur during the next hours. But I am confident that God knows and is in control of my life. My challenge is to trust him.

Prayer: Dear Father, thank you for each day. My time is in your hands. Amen.

Journey to the City – Riding Backwards

Philippians 3:14. *I press on toward the goal for the prize of the heavenly call of God in Christ Jesus.*

Once in late December I rode the local train from my hometown into the city "backwards", since the only available seat faced the opposite direction the train was traveling. For one hour, I looked out the window at where I had been rather than where I was going. My seat offered a different perspective since I saw the other side of the houses and businesses on an otherwise familiar route.

At the end of the year, many of us plan ahead and make New Year's resolutions. My experience on the train reminded me of the importance of looking back as well as looking ahead. I thank God for my loving Christian parents and the Sunday school teachers who provided a wonderful spiritual foundation, and for my current family, church family, and friends who help to nourish my body, soul, and spirit throughout the year. And I give thanks for God's promised presence in the year ahead.

Prayer: Dear Father, thank you for your presence and blessings in our past, present, and future. In Jesus' trustworthy name, Amen.

Journey as an Administrator – Yielding Daily to God

Proverbs 3:21-23. *Have two goals: wisdom – that is, knowing and doing right – and common sense. Don't let them slip away, for they will fill you with living energy, and bring you honor and respect.* (TLB).

As an administrator, I had myriad opportunities and challenges. As a Christian, there were times when I had to ask myself if it was God's will that I exert a potentially negative impact on any of my employees? Prayer for guidance each day was always important. One day there was a particular situation that I needed to address. I was apprehensive; my personal feelings began to overshadow my professional responsibility.

My devotional reading that morning was from Oswald Chambers' *My Utmost for His Highest.* The words were a message of peace from God. "What are you dreading? You are not a coward about it, you are going to face it, but there is a feeling of dread. When there is nothing and no one to help you, say – But the Lord is my Helper, this second, in my present outlook. Are you learning to say things after listening to God's word, or are you saying things and trying to make God's word fit in? Get hold of the Father's say-so, and then say with courage – I will not fear. It does not matter what evil or wrong may be in the way. He has said: I will never leave thee."

Encouraged and supported by this message from God, I was able to meet this one responsibility as well as others that presented themselves on a particular day thereafter.

Prayer: Father, thank you that you fill us with living energy and that you are with us wherever our journeys take us. Amen.

Chambers, Oswald (1956, p 157). *My Utmost for His Highest.* Dodd, Mead & Company, New York.

Journey to Hatboro – Making a Difference

I Kings 19:11-12. *Go out and stand on the mountain before the Lord, for the Lord is about to pass by. Now there was a great wind, so strong that it was splitting mountains and breaking rocks in pieces before the Lord, but the Lord was not in the wind; and after the wind an earthquake, but the Lord was not in the earthquake; and after the earthquake a fire, but the Lord was not in the fire; and after the fire a sound of sheer silence.*

The Old and New Testaments include examples of individuals who made a difference because they stilled themselves through various methods. Queen Esther asked Mordecai to *"'Go, gather all the Jews to be found in Susa, and hold a fast in my behalf, and neither eat or drink for three days, night or day. I and my maids will also fast as you do. After that I will go to the king, though it is against the law, and if I perish, I perish.' Mordecai then went away and did everything as Esther had ordered Him."* (Esther 4:15-17). Esther's actions helped to save the Jews from destruction.

Luke 10:38-42 shared the experiences of two sisters, Martha who was distracted by her many tasks and Mary who sat at the feet of Jesus to listen to him speak. Martha complained that she was left with all the work and wanted the Lord to tell Mary to help her. The Lord's answer was that Mary had chosen the better part, which would not be taken away from her.

The gospel of Matthew describes how Jesus stilled himself at various times. When Jesus was led up by the Spirit into the wilderness to be tempted by the devil, he fasted for 40 days and nights (Matthew 4:1-2). The night before he was betrayed Jesus left his disciples to sit while he went further to pray (Matthew 26:36).

Examples of radical disciples are not limited to the Bible. Twelve years before Hatboro Baptist Church in Hatboro, Pennsylvania was formed in 1835 by six men and sixteen women, Hanna Yerkes moved to the thriving village of Hatborough that was settled in 1715. According to church history (Shannon, 2005), Mrs. Yerkes was "religiously instructed and accustomed to observe the Sabbath." She commented to a friend: "I have located in a heathen land." Her experience made her feel the desire for religious instruction in the village. She suggested, and action was taken, to establish a Sunday school. The principle men and women of the village were engaged as teachers and the Sunday school was opened. After some time, the men became weary of religion and quit the work, leaving it to the ladies to nobly carry on. As a result of this one woman's' vision and action, thousands of children and adults have had the opportunity to know God better at Hatboro Baptist Church over the past years.

Prayer: Dear Father, it is easy to be distracted by many daily tasks and challenges. Help each of us to be still to hear you speak to us in your still small voice, take action, and make a difference in the lives of others. In Jesus' name, Amen.

Reprinted with permission from an online devotion for American Baptist Women's Ministry. November 1, 2006.

Reference: Shannon, D. (2005). *A History of Hatboro Baptist Church*, Hatboro, PA

Journeys Around the House

Journey to the Back Porch – Hidden Beauty

Mark 4:22. *For there is nothing hidden except to be disclosed; nor is anything secret, except to come to light.*

I have a hanging basket of impatiens on my back porch. It hangs from a bracket attached to the back of the house. The flowers bloomed all summer and were enjoyable. One morning I went outside at just that time that the sun shown on that particular area of the porch. Between the basket and the house there was a beautiful spider web gleaming in the sun! This beautiful handiwork was unseen most of the time.

How often this occurs in daily life. There is much hidden beauty around us – in nature and people. We are often unaware of this beauty since we are not looking for it. But, in an unsuspecting moment, we are surprised and thankful when we discover God's beauty all around us.

Prayer: Dear Father, help us to look in all places and to every person for your love and beauty. Amen.

Journey to the Kitchen (1) – Positive Outcomes

Romans 8:28. *We know that all things work together for good for those who love God....*

My friend, the hostess, burned the peas while preparing them for dinner guests. Rather than throw them away, she added multiple condiments and seasonings and came up with a unique-tasting vegetable. When one of the guests commented on the great taste, the hostess replied, "You have to start with burnt peas!"

Sometimes we encounter potentially disastrous circumstances in daily life that are similar to my friend's burnt peas. Rather than give up, we can determine to make something successful from this experience that will bring positive comments from others and allow us to give praise to our heavenly Father.

Prayer: Dear Father, each day brings new experiences. Help us to believe that all things work together for your good. In Jesus' name, Amen.

Journey to the Kitchen (2) – Spiritual Nutrition

Psalm 34:8a. *O taste and see that the Lord is good.*

One aspect of life that many of us consider to be less than ideal is our physical condition or shape. There are books, videos, and businesses that cater to our perceived or real concerns. Nutritional data must be displayed on food packages to keep us informed and help us make wise choices. We can alter our eating habits and exercise routines to build up or trim down our bodies.

Our daily spiritual, as well as physical, nutrition is important for our overall health and growth. Just as we nourish our bodies daily, we need daily nutrition to maintain and enhance our spiritual health. Spiritual nutrients are referenced in the Scriptures. Jesus Christ states, I am the Bread of Life. No one coming to me will ever be hungry again (John 6:35 TLB). The B vitamins that are found in bread and grains are responsible for helping our bodies grow at a normal rate, preventing certain anemias, and building and maintaining body tissue. Partaking of our daily bread of life from God's Word is one way to prevent spiritual anemias.

Galatians 5:22-23 lists the fruits of the spirit: love, joy, peace, long suffering, gentleness, goodness, faith, meekness, temperance. Vitamin C which is found in citrus fruits and juices provides our bodies with nutrients that help us resist infections as well as form proteins that help to support our body structure. The fruits of the Spirit help us to support and build up the body of Christ. The important D vitamins that help to build healthy bones are found in milk and dairy products. The corresponding spiritual nutrients are referenced in 1 Peter 2:2: Like newborn babes, long for the pure spiritual milk, that you may grow up to salvation.

Water is the nutrient that is essential to life, and the lack of it is very evident in everyday life. A wilted plant, brown grass, and dehydrated skin are vivid evidence of the effects that the lack of water has on individuals and nature. John 4:10 states, If only you knew what a wonderful gift God has for you, and who I am, you would ask me for some living water! (TLB).

Bread, fruit, milk, and water are just four foods that are essential for the support of our physical well-being. Our spiritual food is available to us through Jesus Christ when we partake daily from God's Word – our spiritual storehouse- and through fellowship with other Christians.

Prayer: Source of health and strength, you have prepared a table before us. Help us to nourish our souls as well as our bodies every day so that we can serve you. Amen.

Reprinted from *Women at the Well: Meditations on Healing and Wholeness* edited by Mary L. Mild, copyright @ 1996 by Judson Press. Used by permission of Judson Press.

Journey to the Front Yard – New Growth

John 15:5. *I am the vine, you are the branches.*

Nine years ago, when we moved into the 40 year-old house we had just purchased, there was a stump in the front yard. After several years new branches began to grow from all areas of the stump. After years of fertilizing and trimming, we had a beautiful, well-shaped bush. The cut off stump was still there but it was surrounded with healthy new growth.

Although no life was evident the root or vine held the secrets of life and was ready to be reborn with time and care. This stump is an excellent example of the type of rebirth and growth that can take place in our lives. We experience barren times in our lives. But, with God's help, we are able to live and develop new growth.

Prayer: Father, thank you for your loving care that enables us to survive and grow through our experiences. Amen.

Journey to the Garden (1) – Room to Grow

Mark 4:20. *But the good soil represents the hearts of those who truly accept God's message and produce a plentiful harvest for God?... (TLB).*

In the spring I bought two plants in four inch pots. I immediately transplanted the one to a larger pot. Several months later both plants seemed to be healthy and were filled with blossoms but the size of the two was very different. The one plant was about six inches high. The one that had been transplanted was double in height. The smaller one had its growth held back because of its circumstances. I had provided enough water and care for the smaller one to survive but had not given it room to expand and thrive.

At times, I may limit those I love or work with by not providing adequate room for individual expression or growth. Those who are given this opportunity may blossom in ways that I did not expect.

Prayer: Father, thank you for the lessons you teach us each day through the ordinary things of life. Amen.

Journey to the Garden (2) – Vital Nourishment

John 15:5. *I am the vine, you are the branches.*

Once again, the mint that is planted in one corner of the garden had spread in all directions. The familiar green leaves began appearing many inches away from the original plant. These sprigs are able to survive and thrive because of their direct connection with the main source of life.

Scripture compares our relationship with our Heavenly Father like branches are to the vine. Although we may be far away from our home, family, church for various periods of time we are assured that *"…And remember, I am with you always, even to the end of the age."* (Matthew 28:20). This lesson from my garden plant assures me that no matter where I may find myself I am nourished and can thrive as long as I am in contact with my source of eternal life.

Prayer: Dear Father, although I may be far from home and sometimes feel alone, you are ever near to me. Amen

Journey to the Side Porch – A Child's Curiosity

Genesis 1:25. *God made all sorts of wild animals and cattle and reptiles. And God was pleased with what he had done.* (TLB)

I was sitting on my porch reading when I heard my neighbor's son call: "Daddy, Daddy, come look at the worm." The four-year old had discovered one of God's small creations.

"Are there more worms here?" "Why?" "How can they live in the dirt?" "Where did they come from?" The father patiently answered the many questions posed by his son.

For most of us the sighting of a worm would have been an ordinary experience rather than a learning process based on questions and answers. We can learn to appreciate God's handiwork through a child's curiosity.

Prayer: Father, help us to be thankful for all of your creation and to become excited by the ordinary things in life. Amen.

Journey to the Front Porch – The Victor

Ephesians 6:11. *Therefore take up the whole armor of God, so that you may be able to withstand on that evil day and having done everything to stand firm.*

A modern David and Goliath type of battle was taking place outside my screened porch. A small industrious spider snared a locust several times its size in its newly spun web. The spider worked quickly to secure one wing as the locust struggled – unsuccessfully – for freedom. In a few minutes, the small spider had triumphed over a larger locust!

This was a vivid reminder that I can cope and conquer those tasks and responsibilities that seem to be overwhelming obstacles on some days. What is required is swift work to tackle the job and see it through to completion – sometimes in silence and alone – just like the spider. I can rely on God's help to help me meet those challenges that seem as big as Goliath did to David.

Prayer: Dear Father, remind me that you are with me and offer your armor when I have battles to win. Amen.

Journey to the Basement – God's Power

Luke 9:43. *Awe gripped the people as they saw this display of the power of God.* (TLB)

The power of God is evident when one lives along a river. Each fall my husband stored summer items such as lawn furniture, a row boat and several docks in the basement storage area of our home. It took careful planning to fit everything into place.

Several days ago, following a spring thaw, the usually calm river rose to flood height, filling our basement with water and mud. When we were able to get into the area all of the stored items had been tossed about. It was hard to believe that selected items could have been moved by the force of the water since it had taken such effort to fit them into a small area.

The power of God can have the same effect in our lives. The seemingly impossible can be accomplished when we recognize and seek God's power in our daily activities and relationships.

Prayer: Father, help each of us to remember that everything is possible for the person who has faith in you. Amen.

Journey Down the Lane – Guiding Light

Psalm 119:105. *Your word is a lamp to my feet and a light to my path.*

My husband and I spend our summers at our home located along a river. The half-mile stone road that leads to the house is private property and does not have street lights. Except for the lights from the other houses and an occasional outside light, the road is in total darkness by evening. When leaving the house in the early evening to visit friends or share a meal, it is important to take a flashlight or lamp for the return trip home.

Tonight, as we walked the dark road that was illuminated by our small flashlight, I was reminded that God's word is able to provide the same type of light on my pathway.

Prayer: Dear Father, thank you for making us aware of your care for us through the ordinary things of life. Amen.

Journey to the Porch – Sparrows are Important

Luke 12:7. *But even the hairs of your head are all counted. So be not afraid; you are of more value than many sparrows.*

I was sitting on my screened porch reading when I became aware of rustling leaves in the small tree near the porch. A tiny sparrow was fluttering from branch to branch. As quickly as the sparrow came, it was gone. But, it was there long enough to bring to mind the thought for today and remind me that I am important to God. God knows and allows those circumstances that I experience each day. The Lord is with me and protects me as He does all of His creation.

Prayer: Dear Father, thank you for the everyday experiences that remind each of us of your love for us. In Jesus' name, Amen.

Journey to Wholeness – A Clean Heart

Psalm 139:23. *Search me O God, and know my heart: test me and know my thoughts. Create in me a clean heart.*

On a regular basis my computer reminds me that I need to complete a health analysis. The process includes: connecting to the server, downloading updates, gathering information, analyzing the system, and preparing an action list. The desired message I hope to see at the end of the analysis is "passed". This means my computer is clean and no virus was detected.

The scripture thought today applies to our spiritual health. I need to allow God to search my heart, actions, and thoughts each day to make sure that I am following his commandments. I need to confess my sins of omission or commission and ask for God's forgiveness. I also need to read and study my Bible and share my faith with others.

Prayer: Father, please remind me that at times my actions may speak louder than my words. Help me to reflect your love each day to those around me. In Jesus' name, Amen

Journey with Kindness – Gracious Words

Proverbs 25:11. *A word fitly spoken is like apples of gold in a setting of silver.*

The unexpected envelope was addressed to me with a return address from my elected state representative. The card included the words: "I read something nice about you." On the inside of the card was a newspaper photograph and caption that appeared in our local newspaper that announced an award I received. I appreciated this unexpected card and the message it conveyed and also that someone took the time to share.

At times, negative news in the paper and on television outweighs the positive articles. The gracious words and picture I received from an unexpected source inspired me to respond in a similar manner when I read or see something positive about someone I know in the local newspaper or on the news.

Prayer: Father, remind me to share your love with those around me by writing a thank you note, speaking an encouraging word, or performing a random act of kindness as they experience the challenging seasons of life. In Jesus' name, Amen.

Journey Through the Mail – God's Free Gift

Romans 6:23. *For the wages of sin is death, but the free gift of God is eternal life in Christ Jesus our Lord.*

"You were computer selected to receive a free gift. To receive your gift call…. You can win one million dollars cash and a chance to live the way you deserve. Hurry and send in your entry right now. Make your dream come true – send in your entry right away! We want to send you $1,000,000."

The preceding quotes are taken from the mail I received. This offer is for a once-in-a-lifetime opportunity to realize instant wealth. But, I was required to do something to claim my "free gift".

My salvation is a free gift from God. It is not of works, lest anyone should boast. All I had to do was to believe and accept God's gift of eternal life purchased with the blood of his Son, Jesus Christ, on the cross of Calvary.

Prayer: Thank you for sending Your only begotten Son so that all who believe on him may have everlasting life. In Jesus' name. Amen.

Journey to Court – Subject to a Higher Power

Romans 13:1. *Let every person be subject to the governing authorities; for there is no authority except from God, and those authorities that exist have been instituted by God.*

This week I received a subpoena served by an officer of the court that required that I be a witness in a work-related court proceeding the next week. This piece of paper changed multiple business and personal plans for several days. The reason – the power behind the words on the piece of paper that required that I obey.

Many scripture passages tell us of the power of God's words: "God said" and the world was created. Christ said: "Lazarus, come forth." And he that was dead came forth. Christ told the man with a withered hand to "stretch forth your hand" and it was restored whole, like as the other. Our God is all powerful! He had the power to create the world and to create and sustain life. Best of all, He has the power to say "Your sins are forgiven."

Prayer: Father, thank you for being the way, the truth and the life. We trust in your power for all aspects of our lives. Amen.

Journeys with Family and Friends

Journey with Grief – A Special Prayer

Psalm 91:16. *With long life I will satisfy them and show them my salvation.*

My mother-in-law had a long life and died 10 days before her 101st birthday. It is hard to imagine the unbelievable changes and losses that she experienced during those years. One of the losses was the sudden death of her husband at an early age more than 50 years earlier.

Following her death, I sorted through her personal papers and found the following handwritten prayer among some pictures of her husband. I do not know if she or someone else wrote it but it expressed her need at this season of her life.

> Dear Lord, kind Lord, speak to me today,
> Throw a bridge of light across the darkness of today.
> Teach me how to bear a loss I cannot comprehend,
> Help me with my heavy cross until the journey's end.

Prayer: Dear Father, it is sometime overwhelming to attempt to comprehend the illness and loss that many of us, our family, and friends experience each day. Remind us to take time from our busy lives to help each other meet the challenges every day. In Jesus' name, Amen.

Journey with Memories – A Tribute to Mother

II Timothy 1:5. *I am reminded of your sincere faith, a faith that lived first in your grandmother Lois, and your mother Eunice and now, I am sure, lives in you.*

The memories of a loving mother who died following a short terminal illness are captured in the following words I shared during her celebration of life:

> Day by day your guidance and understanding way
> Have helped each one who knew you as they travelled on life's way.
> I always will remember as the years go on and on
> The many happy memories we shared and I now recall.

Prayer: Dear Father, thank you for the blessing of a Christian mother who taught me to love and trust in you. In Jesus' name, Amen.

Journey on a Sailplane – Total Dependence on God

John 15:5. *…because apart from me you can do nothing.*

My husband and I went soaring in a sailplane. This aircraft has no power of its own. A tow plane pulls out in front of the plane, a rope is attached that carries the plane aloft. Once airborne, the sailplane is released for the pilot to maneuver it on its own while thermals created by the warmth of the sun keep it aloft. The flight is beautiful, peaceful, and too short as gravity slowly draws the plane towards the landing site.

I was reminded through this experience of how similar I am to this sailplane. I am dependent on an external and eternal power source to provide me with life and the energy to accomplish everything. When I am filled with God's powers I can do all things through Christ who strengthens me (Phil.4:13).

Prayer: Dear Father, thank you for your Almighty Power that gives eternal life through faith in you and the energy to meet our daily challenges. Amen.

Journey for a New Car – Wrong Assumptions

Proverbs 20:29. *The glory of youths is their strength but beauty of the aged is their gray hair.*

My husband and I visited a new car dealer. During our visit the salesman said:" The rear doors have safety locks that will protect your grandchildren." His words startled me. We both have gray hair but we have no children, nor grandchildren.

Another time, a young newspaper reporter described her companions in a hot air balloon ride as "two 60 year-old women." I happened to be one of those women and I was not as old as I appeared to this young reporter.

On another occasion a young man at a fast food restaurant quoted me the senior citizen price for a cup of coffee. I thanked him and asked how he knew I was a senior citizen. He told me I looked as old as his mother!

Each of these individuals made assumptions based on general appearances and assumptions rather than facts. In our daily encounters, do we make assumptions about those we meet – family, friends, co-workers, or strangers based on our own expectations, beliefs or past experiences rather than facts?

Prayer: Dear Father, help us to make wise decisions based on facts rather than on assumptions. In Jesus' name, Amen.

Journey on a Bicycle – Switching Gears

Psalm 46:10a. *Be still and know that I am God!*

I rode a one-speed bicycle for the first 50 years of my life. I resisted a multi-speed bicycle; insisting that I needed the exercise. Several years ago I received a three-speed bike for my birthday. I discovered that I can cover the same distance with less effort when I shift gears. The hard work can be eased when I pause and shift gears.

This same principle applies to other areas of my life. Many time the tasks become easier when I pause rather than rushing and struggling to accomplish multiple responsibilities in a given timeframe. I know the Lord is with me and that I should be still – slow down – shift gears- and know that the Lord is God.

Prayer: Dear Father, thank you for the assurance that you are with me at all times in all areas of life. Remind me to be still and know that you are my God. Amen.

Journey in the Dark – Let Your Light Shine

Matthew 5:14,16. *You are the light of the world…In the same way, let your light shine before others, so that they may see your good works and give glory to your Father in heaven.*

During the day a lightning bug found its way into the house. I was not aware that this occurred until I was in bed with the lights out. On a periodic basis, there was a flashing light in various areas of the bedroom. This tiny bug was able to arouse my attention in a quiet, but bright way.

A song I learned many years ago included the words: "This little light of mine, I'm going to let it shine." I also read somewhere: "If you can't be a shining star, at least twinkle a little." Both of these suggestions remind us that we are to be light in a world filled with darkness.

Prayer: Dear Father, thank you that you are the source of our light. May others see your light shining through us. In Jesus' name, Amen.

Journey with a Child – God's Wireless Connection

Jeremiah 33:3: *Call to me and I will answer you and will tell you great and hidden things you have not known.*

A relative explained the death of the 4 year old's grandfather by telling her "pop-pop" went to live with God. The child's immediate response was: "Does God have a telephone so I can call him?" The child was referring to the familiar telephone she used to call her grandfather on a regular basis.

God has a direct, wireless connection–prayer. We do not need any type of device and there is never a busy signal, call waiting, or recorded message. God knows us by name and invites us to call on him and he will answer and show us great and mighty things.

Prayer: Dear Father, thank you that each of us has the privilege of direct access to you through prayer. In Jesus' name, Amen.

Journey Through Searching – One Lost Coin

Luke 15:9. *Rejoice with me, for I have found the coin that I had lost.*

I own a one-cent piece dated 1845. This coin has sentimental value because of its history. It also is a conversation piece.

One night I noticed the coin was missing from my change purse. I searched my handbag for it without success. I remembered the purse has fallen from the car seat earlier in the week. Like the woman in the parable I lit a lamp and searched every nook and cranny until I found the missing coin.

Scriptures tells us that every detail of life is important to our Heavenly Father: the hairs of our head are numbered; His eye is on the sparrow, and there is joy in the presence of the angels over one sinner that repents. The details and concerns of my life are important to my Father in heaven.

Prayer: Father, thank you for your faithfulness to us in both the big and small details of life. In Jesus' name, Amen.

Journey for Clothes – At All Times

I Corinthians 10:31 *…or whatever you do, do everything for the glory of God.*

I bought an item at the local store that was too large for a bag so the clerk put it in my cart after I paid for it. As I left the store, a security guard said: "I'm sure you paid for the item in the cart but I need to see your receipt." As an afterthought, the guard said: "Just in case I'm being watched to see if I am doing my job."

Today's scripture reminds me that whatever I do must glorify God. My responsibilities need to be carried out at all times, not just when I am being observed or believe I might be observed. All of us are to be imitators of Christ.

Prayer: Dear Father, each of us has unlimited opportunities to bring glory to you every day. Help us to meet the challenges each day. In Jesus' name, Amen.

Journey to the Hospital – A New Heart

Ezekiel 11:19. *A new heart I will give you, and a new spirit I will put within; and I will remove from your body the heart of stone and give you a heart of flesh.*

A friend was in the hospital, on the waiting list for a heart transplant. The call that a healthy, donor heart was immediately available came at 7 PM. While my friend was prepared for surgery, his family waited for the helicopter to arrive at the hospital with his new heart. His wife later said, "It was a moment I will never forget- seeing the doctors getting out of the helicopter carrying the cooler, looking up, seeing us, and giving us the thumbs-up sign." The surgery was successful and my friend was able to return home to enjoy his family and resume limited activities at his church.

Most of us do not need a physical heart transplant. But, as today's scripture states, we need to have our hearts of stone replaced by hearts of flesh; in other words, our hearts need to be softened and nourished by the Holy Spirit.

Prayer: God, thank you for Jesus who died and rose again to give us new spiritual hearts. Thank you for a new life in you. Amen.

Journey with New Birth – A Child is Born

Luke 2:11. *To you is born this day in the city of David, a Savior, who is the Messiah, the Lord.*

Our local hospital plays a short lullaby over the loud speaker system throughout the hospital each time a baby is born. This tune alerts staff, patients, and visitors of the new arrival. The music sometimes generates questions from visitors who are not familiar with this method of announcing births. This morning I was at the hospital for several hours in my volunteer role and heard the lullaby twice. When I hear this lullaby I take the opportunity to thank God for the miracle of birth and to pray for God's blessing on the new baby, mother and family.

More than 2000 years ago Jesus was born in Bethlehem. His birth was not announced with a soft lullaby but with a multitude of the heavenly host, praising God and saying: "*Glory to God in the highest heaven, and on earth peace among those whom he favors.*" (Luke 2:13-14).

Prayer: Dear Father, thank you for the birth of your Son, Jesus Christ the Lord. Remind us to give you praise for salvation through Him and for eternal life by believing on Him. Amen.

Journey as a Caregiver – Multiple Challenges

Psalm 46:10a. *Be still and know that I am God.*

During a recent meeting the leader asked each of us to repeat Psalm 46:10a five times. Each time we were to leave off a word or words and repeat the new shorter sentence.

> Be still and know that I am God.
> Be still and know that I am.
> Be still and know.
> Be still.
> Be.

Once a week I serve as a volunteer on an inpatient hospice. My volunteer responsibilities, in addition to assisting the nursing staff with patient care, are to give mouth care with cold water swabs and apply a soothing gel to dry lips. Additional responsibilities are to provide companionship for patients and families, be a good listener, and show compassion. Many time, all that I am asked to do is to "be". I sit in silence with a patient who is unresponsive, hold a hand or listen to family members as they share memories of their loved ones. At these times, what is required of me is to "be", not to do anything but just to "be", or according to the dictionary, to exist with the patient and family.

November is National Caregivers' Recognition Month. Women, children, and other family members of various ages care for family and friends, many on a 24-hour a day, seven days a week basis. There are times when caregivers would appreciate the time and opportunity to be still. Many of us are accustomed to, and comfortable with, "doing" rather than "being".

We are quick to offer to prepare meals or run errands. But, an offer to sit with a healthy newborn or child with physical or mental challenges or older adult who no longer remembers our name is a special gift. The challenge for each of us is to be comfortable to just "be". We do not need to talk, listen to music, or watch television. To "be" is many times "just what the doctor ordered."

Prayer: Dear Father, many of your children's lives are filled with multiple challenges. I pray for comfort, strength, and patience as they meet their responsibilities with your help and the support of family and friends. Remind me to ask: Who do I know who would benefit from my offer to "be"? Amen.

Reprinted with permission from an online devotion for American Baptist Women's Ministry. November 2, 2006.

Journeys by Those with Physical Challenges

Journey to a Doctor's Office – Honest Words

Matthew 26:73. *Certainly you are one of them; for your accent betrays you.*

I visited a medical specialist for a diagnostic test. During the interview I responded to a specific question: "I do not take any meds." The doctor asked if I worked in a hospital. I said, "No, why?" He told me I used the word "meds" instead of pills. Without realizing it my speech conveyed the fact that I am a nurse and familiar with medical jargon.

An anonymous poem written on the inside cover of the Bible I received for high school graduation in 1954 includes the following words: "You tell what you are by the way you walk; by the things of which you delight to talk." Each day, in some manner, our actions and speech betray us. Do those around us know that we are Christians by our walk and talk?

Prayer: "O Lord, help my words to be gracious and tender today, for tomorrow I may have to eat them. Amen." (Anonymous prayer).

Journey to a Hospital (1) – Coronary Care

Proverbs 4:23. *Keep your heart with all vigilance; for from it flows the springs of life.*

My mother was in the coronary care unit attached to a monitoring device that registered her heart activity at the nurses' station. When mother moved one of the electrodes became detached. Mother asked me to reattach the device before the nurse knew it was off. Of course there was no time for this since the separation registered at the desk and the nurses responded within seconds.

This hospital experience illustrates our relationship to God. We sometimes stray from our life support system. Our Heavenly Father knows what is happening to His children at all times. He is always ready to respond to our needs. Sometime, the answer arrives before we have taken the time to call on Him for help.

Prayer: Dear Father, remind us through our daily experiences that each day is a gift from you to be enjoyed. Amen,

My mother, Florence Dickert

Journeys with God – Page 98

Journey to a Hospital (2) – Trauma Alert

Matthew 25:13. *Keep awake therefore, for you know neither the day nor the hour.*

Attention: Trauma Alert – Level II ETA [expected time of arrival] is 1 minute. This announcement was heard on the speaker system throughout the hospital where I am a nurse. The message alerted the members of the trauma team throughout the hospital that someone with serious injuries would arrive in the emergency department in one minute. Identified professionals would go to the emergency room and use their professional skills in an attempt to save a life. The team had advance warning of the pending arrival and time to respond. The individual who was to receive the care probably had no warning of the pending accident or medical emergency.

Scripture states that now is the day of salvation. Now is the time to prepare for eternity since we do not know what the future holds, nor when Christ will return. Now is also the time to do those important things that we often put off until a more convenient time.

Prayer: Father, thank you for providing for our spiritual health, our salvation through your Son, Jesus. Also, thank you for the skills and dedication of the various professionals who tend to our physical health. In Jesus' name, Amen.

Journey with Blindness – Walk by Faith

II Corinthians 5:7. *For we walk by faith, not by sight.*

One Sunday the deacons served communion. The service went smoothly with no interruptions or mishaps. My reason for sharing this fact is that I know that one of the deacons is blind. This deacon served to the choir bread and wine without fanfare or special treatment. By her own predetermined method, she was able to reach a certain spot on the altar, turn to her left and carry out her duties while her faithful dog sat nearby. Her silent action was a powerful second sermon that day on how to view all potential problems as opportunities.

How often do we make excuses when we should be taking advantage of each opportunity?

Prayer: Dear God, help each one of us to view daily problems as opportunities to honor you. In Jesus' name, Amen

Journey with Arthritis – Helping Hands

Psalm 88:9. *O Lord, I reach my pleading hands to you for mercy.* (TLB)

"I can wear gloves again!" For most of us the simple task of putting on gloves does not represent a conscious act. But, for my 70-year old friend whose hands were crippled with arthritis; this act was an impossible task.

My friend lived alone by choice. Her crippled hands made many tasks such as using a can opener, carrying a utensil, or getting dressed, very difficult. I was her visiting nurse and she called me to request a visit after I had not seen her for several months. When I arrived it was immediately apparent that she had two beautiful – not deformed – hands as the result of recent reconstructive surgery. Her first words: "I can wear gloves again!" reminded me of my many daily blessings and made me appreciate the small things in life that I so often take for granted.

Prayer: Dear God, thank you for healthy hands to help others each day. In Jesus' name, Amen.

Journey with Disability – Sturdy Vessels

Isaiah 43:2. *...When you walk through fire you shall not be burned, and the flame shall not consume you.*

One morning I fried bacon and spooned the remaining hot fat into an empty six-ounce plastic juice can. As the hot fat touched the can it began to take on a different appearance. The sides bulged and it shrank in height. Although it changed in appearance, the can continue to function as a useful container.

Many people we meet each day have experienced the extreme heat or pressures of daily life. Like my plastic container, their physical appearances may have changed due to age, disability, illness, or circumstances. Some individuals retain the capacity to carry out their responsibilities and maintain useful lifestyles. Others need help during time of pressure. When we are sensitive to the needs of those around us we can provide support during stressful times.

Prayer: Help us to be alert to the needs of others who are experiencing the stresses of daily life. In Jesus' name, Amen.

Journey with Grief – Do it Now!

Philippians 2:4. *Let each of you look not to your own interests, but to the interests of others!*

The teen-aged child of a friend of mine was killed in an automobile accident. Two days ago this friend came to my mind several times during the day. I sat down and wrote a note letting her know that I was thinking about her and offering support during her time of grief. I took the letter to the mailbox.

A few days later I had a telephone call from a mutual friend who told me that the day my note arrived was an extremely difficult day for our friend. It was the birthday of her late son.

Once again, I believe God had directed me to do one small deed – now! The value of a short note expressing concern, written on inexpensive note paper, inserted in an envelope with a stamp attached, and mailed to a special person was invaluable.

Prayer: Father, help us to be sensitive to the needs of those around us and to respond in loving ways that honor you. Amen.

Journey after Surgery – Silent Partner

James 1:19. *...let everyone be quick to listen, slow to speak, slow to anger....*

Following surgery on his vocal cords, my husband was temporarily unable to speak or whisper. All of his communicating was done in sign language or writing. I quickly learned to pose questions that could be answered by a nod of the head or with one word. At times, one word was all that he needed to write to convey a thought to me. At other times, a sentence did not get the message across to me. The vocal inflections were missing.

This temporary muteness increased my appreciation of the difficulties experienced by individuals with speech or hearing challenges and the resulting effect this has on family members. It also made me aware of the importance of all of the senses that God had given to us.

Prayer: Dear God, help us to have patience with those we meet who have all types of physical challenges. Amen.

Journey with Terminal Illness – Seasons of Life

Ecclesiastes 3:1-2. *For everything there is a season, and a time for every matter under heaven: a time to be born, and a time to die.*

As a nurse, I am accustomed to initiating discussions about a living will/advance directive with patients to determine the type of care that they prefer if they become incapacitated. Does the patient have a living will? Does it include Do Not Resuscitate instructions? The conscious decision of an individual to consider the advantages and disadvantages of life-support systems and to provide written instructions to family and professional caregivers is very important when a healthcare crisis situation arises.

My Mother was an eighty-four-year-old widow who was always busy; going out to breakfast, lunch, or dinner, shopping, taking a trip with friends, attending a church activity. It was sometimes hard to find her home unless I made an appointment. Her latest hobby was learning to knit. She loved to care for her home and yard. The telephone call from my cousin informing me that Mother was not feeling well, followed by her emergency admission to a hospital with a short-term terminal illness, was unexpected.

Fortunately, mother had communicated her wishes to me and her physician. Her conscious act to live in my home, in familiar surroundings with family, until life ended, without the assistance of life-support measures, provided the opportunity to share some of the most precious moments of a lifetime.

Prayer: Great Healer of body and soul, remind us that to everything there is a season, even a time to die. Give us the courage to consider and record our wishes, whatever these may be, since they are an important aspect of health and wholeness for those we love. Amen.

Reprinted from *Women at the Well: Meditations on Healing and Wholeness* edited by Mary L. Mild, copyright © 1996 by Judson Press. Used by permission of Judson Press.

Journey with Facts – Beauty is Skin Deep

Job 10:11. *You gave me skin and flesh and knit together bones and sinews.*

Have you ever stopped to think about your skin? Skin is that amazing, soft, protective covering for the body that has many characteristics. Skin mirrors our general state of health. Our face may flush from a fever, appear pale when we do not feel well, have a rosy glow from cold weather, or blush when we are embarrassed. Skin has other wonderful characteristics such as being waterproof, offering protection from bacteria, containing our body fluids, and having the ability to heal itself whether the wound results from a tiny pinprick, a paper cut, or a major surgical procedure.

Skin has another important function – the sense of touch. A superficial burn from a hot iron or stove causes us to withdraw quickly. The loving touch of a spouse, child, or friend adds pleasure to our day. The sense of touch provides the opportunity for each one to reach out to others during times of health, illness, and unexpected circumstances. We can also experience the sensation of touch for ourselves.

Prayer: Thank you, loving Creator, for making me so wonderfully complex! It is amazing to think about. Your handiwork is marvelous – and how well I know it. Amen.

Reprinted from *Women at the Well: Medications on Health and Wholeness* edited by Mary L. Mild, copyright © 1996 by Judson Press. Used by permission of Judson Press.

Journey with Weights – To be Free

Hebrews 12:1. *Let us strip off anything that slows us down or holds us back, and especially those sins that wrap themselves so tightly around our feet and trip us up, and let us run with patience the particular race that God has set before us.* (TLB).

As part of a prescribed exercise program for an injured shoulder I attached weights to my one arm. The purpose was to increase the resistance, thereby making the prescribed exercises more difficult to accomplish. After months of diligent adherence to the prescribed program, I regained full range of motion of my arm and shoulder and was able to set aside the weight and resume normal activities. Many times, as I faithfully carried out my routine several times a day, I thought about the above Scripture verse and looked forward to the day that I could lay aside the strapped on weight.

At times, each of us carries around physical or emotional weights that result from myriad circumstances, including health, employment, or finances. It is very easy to get sidetracked as we deal with our daily responsibilities and challenges. We need to spend time in prayer, meditation, and fellowship with other Christians in order to continue on the path that God has set for us.

Prayer: God of steadfastness and encouragement, help us to cast all of our cares on you, for you care for us. Amen.

Reprinted from *Women at the Well: Meditations on Health and Wholeness* edited by Mary L. Mild, copyright © 1996 by Judson Press. Used by permission of Judson Press.

Part II – Reflections

Childhood Memories

My childhood memories of the 1940s and 1950s include many activities that are now outdated. Spring housecleaning was an annual event! The rugs were hung on the outside clothesline and the dust removed with a wire beater. The sheer curtains were washed and delivered to a neighbor who attached them to a stretcher frame with needlelike projections for drying. They required no ironing prior to rehanging. The living room and bedroom furniture were rearranged. The metal coil springs for the beds (no box springs) were cleaned with soap and water and a special brush.

The kitchen tasks included going to the store with ration coupons to purchase a limited supply of selected items. White margarine was made to look like butter by adding a packet of yellow coloring or by squeezing a capsule contained inside the plastic bag with the margarine.

There were no "throw-away" items. Umbrellas with broken spokes were put aside until "Charlie the umbrella man" came to town and made needed repairs. On a regular basis, my mother, aunts, and I went to a local farmer to select printed feed bags (the feed for the animals was packaged in heavy cotton bags) to make our dresses. The challenge was to find several bags with the same design to have enough material to make a dress. My mother, grandmother, and aunts taught me to sew, knit, crochet and embroider.

Today the wire rug beater, washboard, and other long unused items are ornaments in my home rather than useful tools. But these memories remind me that my mother, grandmother, and aunts were wonderful role models who instilled the love of Jesus in my life during my early years. Although the women in my family did not have many of the conveniences that I enjoy today and were tired from doing the many chores, they made time for daily Bible reading and prayer plus attendance at church services several time a week. Bible reading and prayer were important aspects of the busy days and nights. These women displayed many of the wonderful attributes noted in Proverbs 31:10-31. I am thankful for the women in my life who taught me about God's love in my early life and served as examples throughout their lives.

Reprinted from *Vital Woman*. 5 (20):10-11. June 2007. American Baptist Women's Ministries. Used with permission.

My Parents, Florence and Roger Dickert

The Patchwork Quilt

2 Timothy 1:5. *I am reminded of your sincere faith, a faith that lived first in your grandmother Lois, and your mother Eunice, and now, I am sure lives in you.*

One of my earliest memories of my grandmother was when she served as hostess at the frequent quilting bees that took place in our home where my grandmother lived. My grandmother (Alice), mother (Florence), aunts, and other women from our church were always busy with some aspect of quilting. Later in her life, due to health problems, grandmother's participation was limited to activities that she could do while confined to her bed. She kept busy cutting and hand-sewing various shapes from multicolored pieces of fabric that others would sew together into the larger piece to be quilted.

When I was 15 years old my grandmother handcrafted a wedding ring pattern heirloom quilt for my hope chest. During my years of marriage the quilt was on a shelf to preserve it rather than on display in my home.

I remembered my quilt when the planning committee for the National Health Ministries Association's annual meeting (Valley Forge, Pennsylvania, 2003) asked members to loan quilts to be used as the backdrop in the hotel ballroom where the programs would be held. I loaned my quilt to the committee. The first time I walked into the ballroom I was thrilled to see my quilt positioned to the left of the speaker's podium.

Throughout the conference a photojournalist took pictures of attendees and events. Photographs were displayed during the conference and attendees could order photographs by placing the corresponding number assigned to each photograph on the order form. I selected one photograph that included a portion of my heirloom. I was surprised and overwhelmed when I recorded the number of the photograph I ordered – 424. The number of the photograph corresponded with the house number where my parents lived from 1933 when they were married until 1988 when my mother died, and where my grandmother cut, sewed, and helped to quilt my heirloom so many years ago.

This experience reminded me of the wonderful memories I have of my maternal grandmother (the only grandparent I knew) who died in 1951, my mother who died in 1988, and the Christian faith that lived in them and now in me.

Reprinted from *Vital Woman Magazine*. American Baptist Women's Ministries. June 2005. 3 (2):8, 9. Used with permission.

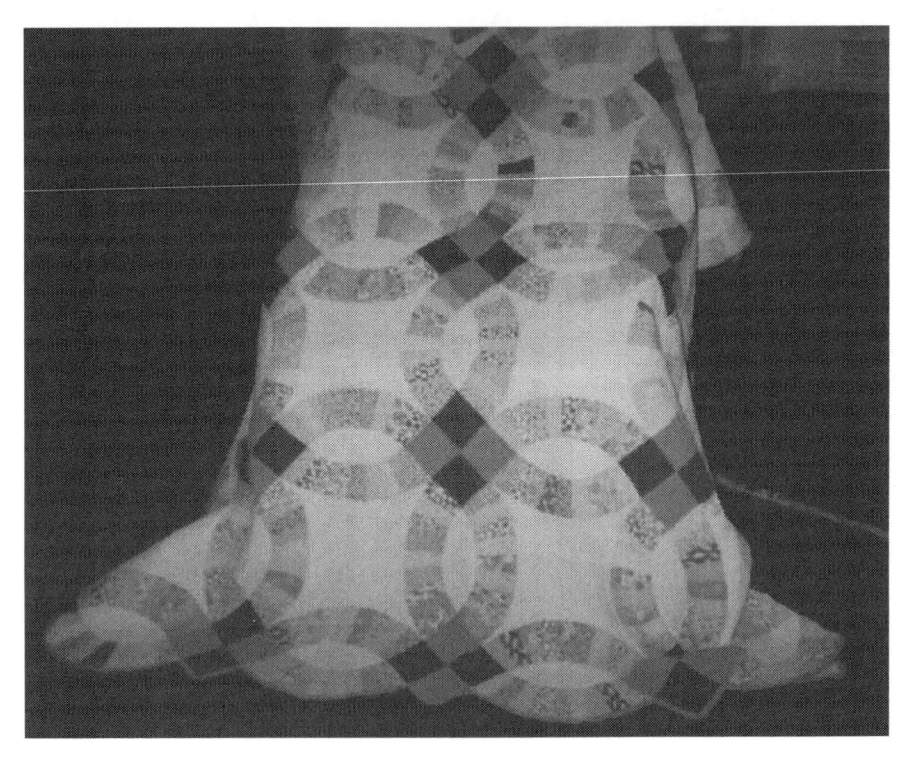

Wedding Ring Quilt

My mother, Florence Dickert

My grandmother, Alice Hertzog

Journeys with God – Page 115

The View from the Other Side of the Bed

In 1957, one month after graduating from nursing school and taking my state board of nursing examination, I had orthopedic surgery. I soon found out what it was like to be a bedbound patient rather than a nurse.

When a person has emergency surgery he or she has one advantage: not having a lot of time to be concerned about the pending operation. The same could not be said for the planned orthopedic surgery I faced at age 21. As a new registered nurse, I had specific ideas of the circumstances that should exist so that life would be "right" for me. I had hopes, dreams, and aspiration, none of which included spending several months in a plaster broom stick cast (from neck to knees) recovering from surgery that I had kept putting off.

When I think of faith I refer to my belief in God. But the dictionary also defines faith as "confidence or dependence on a person, statement or thing as trustworthy." I experienced these aspects of faith during my months as a patient. Confidence in a person was put to the test when the surgeon told me that I had procrastinated long enough. After much deliberation, I signed the surgical permit. But giving informed consent was just the beginning, an act requiring just a few seconds. The surgery would take a few hours. My apprehension came from the thought of the months of recovery. How would I occupy my time? Would all go well with surgery? Would I be able to walk again? Would I be an inconvenience to my family who cared for me during my recuperation? What about my career?

In addition to the medical professionals, I had great faith in my family who became my excellent, private duty caregivers. They placed my hospital bed on the first floor in the dining room so that I would not miss anything. My family prepared and served meals, attended to my physical needs, and included me in activities. For instance, from my bed I helped bake cookies. My family turned me onto my abdomen, sideways in bed, and placed the piano bench next to the bed so that I could mix cookie dough on the makeshift table.

My friends were faithful visitors. My guest book included 444 signatures. Of course, everyone had to sign the book each time he or she came! The postman even delivered mail addressed creatively as "Miss Plaster Cast". Since my home was about three blocks from my church my Sunday school teacher often brought my class to my home so that I would not miss the study and fellowship. The youth group also held several meetings and socials at my home.

My faith in the community was also evident during these months. Many people I did not know donated blood for my benefit. I had confidence in the telephone operator (yes, we had one in our small town) and the police and fire departments who knew that I was incapacitated. Fortunately, I never had to use their services, but it lessened my fears to know they were available if needed.

Finally, I had faith in myself. First, that I had made the right decision and, second, that my legs would hold my weight, I would have balance when I was allowed to walk, and I would eventually return to work.

Now, years later, the physical ordeal is almost forgotten. But this experience helped me in my personal, professional, and spiritual life. I appreciate the little things that a patient requests such as to have a tray table moved closer. A glass of water or box of tissues that is just out of reach is of no value. I also learned that time passes more slowly for the patient than for the nurse. I might have missed these valuable lessons if I had not been on the receiving end of the caring process early in my career.

Reprinted from *Vital Woman*. 5 (3):8-9. October 2007. American Baptist Women's Ministries. Used with permission.

Up, Up and Away!

As a teenager, I sat on the front porch of my home in Emmaus, PA in the early evening and watched hot air balloons drift across the distant sky. I determined that one day I would experience such a ride. Some years ago, I bought two tickets for a ride for a birthday present for my husband in order to fulfill my dream. I was surprised when he refused to go on the ride but agreed to be part of the chase crew. I therefore invited a coworker to be my guest.

After two cancelled appointments due to unfavorable weather conditions, one beautiful summer evening we arrived at our takeoff location. The wicker gondola rested on the ground while the pilot and a young couple (who received their tickets as a wedding present) who would also be on the ride inflated the balloon. When all was ready, the four passengers and the pilot climbed into the wicker gondola and we were off! The 360-degree aerial view was spectacular as we drifted above streams, houses, farms, fields, and folks waving to say hello or to drive us from their property.

After a wonderful ride of approximately one hour, the pilot sighted a plowed field where he determined he could land. As the balloon descended, he prepared all of us for the landing, hands and knees in proper position. In hindsight, perhaps I should have asked how a flat-bottomed basket would land! The landing, although slightly bumpy, started off well. But when an unexpected gust of wind picked up the gondola and balloon, we were aloft again, a few feet off the ground for a short distance, before we landed the second time. This time the passengers were not prepared, and the four of us crumpled to the bottom of the gondola. The end result included a fractured leg for my coworker, serious bruises, and one bloody nose for the rest of us.

To add to the drama, a man immediately came sprinting toward the gondola after we landed. The pilot commented to the rest of us that he was hoping the man was coming to help rather than to scold him for landing on his property! Thankfully, the man did offer his help rather than reprimand us when he arrived.

A few days later my coworker brought a newspaper to work that included a photograph and description of our experience. It turned out that the young woman passenger was a writer for the newspaper and shared her experience with her readers. My friend and I had to laugh as we read her description of us as "two older women who stood by and watched" as she and her husband helped the pilot at the beginning of our adventure. "Older women," indeed!

Proverbs 20:29 says, "The glory of young men is their strength, gray hair the splendor of the old." To one fellow passenger during my hot air balloon experience, my hair color gave the impression that I was old rather than prematurely gray at that time. I took comfort in the words of that Scripture – she may have seen me as older, but in the hot air balloon (despite the bruises), I certainly felt splendor!

Reprinted from *Vital Woman.* 4 (1):12. February 2006. American Baptist Women's Ministries. Used with permission.

One Special Family

During my years as a home care nurse I had the opportunity to meet thousands of patients and families under various circumstances in several countries. One unforgettable experience was during a Soviet-American study tour in 1982.

It was twilight as I stood on the twelfth-floor balcony of the Intourist Hotel in Yerevan, Armenia. In the distance was Mount Ararat in Turkey, but below, on three sides of my hotel was a shantytown. I could see inside some of the homes since the sidewalls did not reach the roofs. Some homes had electricity. A common pump served as the water supply.

Four nurses and I, members of a public health nursing tour of the Soviet Union, walked through this devastated area on our way back to our hotel after a tour of the city. Our guide told us that this area of the city was scheduled for reconstruction, but the residents did not want to relocate. We met nine-year old David (not his real name) playing near our hotel. He spoke a few words of English and invited the five of us to come to his home for coffee. We arranged a 6 PM date for that evening.

We arrived late but David was waiting. We walked through narrow paths, past women doing laundry and washing dishes in tubs outside their shelters, up several walkways, and down steps to a small doorway that led to a small entryway. There we met David's family. His father was eating his evening meal of cucumber, anise, and a potato alone at a small table in a porch-like area. David led us into the house through a modest bedroom and into the living room that included a bed, a table, chairs, a television, an aquarium, an oriental rug hanging on one wall, a china closet filled with dishes, cases filled with books, and a dresser with a mirror. A lace curtain on the only window and a simple ceiling light completed the room. We marveled at how this family had created an oasis amid all the external squalor!

We communicated using an English grammar book belonging to David and his sisters, our Russian-English dictionary, and the few words of Russian we knew. We learned that David's father was a mechanic and that they understood that we were nurses. Some neighbors came to meet us as well.

Although we had been told to avoid drinking the local water, we sipped the thick black coffee that David's mother served us. One nurse presented candy to David's mother. A daughter took a dish from the china closet and placed the candy in it to serve to the guests – us.

Before we left, we all agree to pose for a picture. David's mother motioned for me to wait while she took off her apron and brushed her hair. As we stood with these new friends and shook hands, tears filled my eyes. These people, this family in particular, whom I would never see again, seemed happy, content, and eager to entertain using the meager possessions in their humble home.

I experienced many emotions during my visit, including admiration, warmth, pity, and frustration. I thought about the time I complained about trivial matters that seemed immaterial at a time like this. I gained a deeper appreciation for my personal faith, political freedom, well-stocked supermarket shelves and one-stop shopping, running water, sanitary facilities, fast food restaurants, excellent health care facilities, and wonderful opportunities I have as a professional nurse in the United States.

Reprinted from *Vital Woman*. 4 (2):14. June 2006. American Baptist Women's Ministries. Used with permission.

"Hello, I Think I Know You."

"Hello, I think I know you. When did you start to work here?" Although I visited Jean, a 78-year-old widow, on a weekly, sometimes daily, basis for 12 years she greeted me the same way many times. Jean had symptoms related to benign tremors and dementia. Her husband was a wonderful caregiver until his death. Their only son had died as an infant.

It became evident soon after her husband's death that Jean could not live alone in her home with her two beloved dogs. Health and safety factors associated with her physical status made it necessary to seek alternate care.

Jean's sister had power-of-attorney and was able to arrange for Jean to live in a personal care facility where Jean had worked for years prior to her retirement. Jean knew many of the staff and some residents. Her new residence offered a skilled nursing facility in addition to personal care should she need a higher level of care in the future. The staff in the facility was wonderful and Jean seemed to enjoy her years in personal care.

Some of my visits with Jean were on Sunday afternoons when local churches conducted weekly services for the residents. During one of these services the speaker gave each person who attended a "yellow fluffy". The fluffy was made from several strands of yellow yarn that were tied into a soft bow that the residents and visitors could take with them. The speaker reminded the residents that whenever they were alone, felt alone, or needed someone or something to hold onto, the yellow fluffy would be nearby. Many months later, the yellow fluffy was in Jean's room. Mine was on my bedside table. This small piece of yarn reminded me of God's presence at all times and his promise in "I will never leave you nor forsake you".

Jean fell and broke her hip. She had to be transferred to the skilled nursing facility after she returned home from the hospital. Once again, the staff was wonderful. In addition to the quality nursing care she received, the activities director took the time and effort to attach pictures of Jean's favorite dogs to the ceiling above Jean's bed so that she could see them when she was awake but unable to get out of bed. Aromatherapy was accomplished through a scented cotton ball taped to her blouse. Her fractured hip healed but she became more debilitated and disoriented. She no longer had her usual greeting when I visited with her. Her constant companion was her favorite large stuffed bear.

My visits with Jean ended when she died peacefully in her sleep. I miss my visits with her. I did not work at the facility where Jean was a guest. But, Jean did know me. She was my older sister.

My sister, Jean Gerhart

Qualities – Past and Present

In the Past

> I knew a young man who was kind
> Who many times came to my mind.
> We walked and we talked and
> It was quite a delight
> To have dinner with him by candlelight.
> He repaired broken items and offered advice
> He also brought flowers that were oh so nice.
> Our initial friendship turned into love.
> We married.

At Present

> I know a mature man who is kind
> Who is daily a part of my life.
> Although our life style has changed
> And some hair has turned gray
> Some things will always remain.
> He continues to fix things and offer advice
> We still have our dinners by candlelight
> But we also take time for much more.
> A bicycle ride in the country
> A visit with longtime friends
> Private moments at a special retreat
> Viewing a quiet river at sunset
> Sharing our bread with some friendly geese.
> Why do I think that my husband is special?
> The answer is easy and clear.
> He provides me with many fond memories
> One for each day of the year.

Written by Marilyn D. Harris for Charlie and Marilyn's 25th wedding anniversary on February 8, 1994.

Wedding Day, February 8, 1969

Charlie

Marilyn and Charlie

My Fondest Memories of Nursing

In 2014 I celebrated my 60th years since I embarked on my nursing career. My professional career has been wonderful. I had many opportunities and challenges that are a lasting part of my own history and memories. My administrative responsibilities gave me the opportunity to be innovative and creative, to establish and attain professional and personal goals, enjoy achievements, share my ideas and opinions through publications and host and visit international colleagues.

I will share just a few of the many memories that inspired me during my 60 year career as a community/home care/hospice nurse, supervisor and administrator.

- During the 1960s I was a staff visiting nurse. Many times, there were small children in the homes where I provided care to patients of all ages. Two of my favorite memories are the hand-drawn cards I received from the children I met in patient's home. Both children drew their impressions of a nurse on the front of their notes. One child included my maiden name on her drawing. The other child addressed me as "nerssi". I remember the homes and the circumstances associated with both of these children. It was my hope that the children's early experiences with a nurse may have influenced their choice of a career. I know that one of the children chose nursing as a career.

- One of my first patients in 1961 was a baby boy who was born with Down's syndrome and numerous medical conditions. He and his family faced many challenges. I continued to send him a birthday card for many years and his mother sent me a note and a current picture. In July 2001, I received my annual picture of "Bob" at his 40th birthday party. I lost contact when his living arrangements changed but he and his loving family remain in my memories.

- On many occasions family members took the time to write personal thank you notes to me or to my supervisor. Fortunately, my supervisor gave me the original or copies of these letters that I included in my "memory books". The following excerpts are from four letters:

- There is no possible way that I can express my appreciation for what you did for my mother, the happiness I know you brought her each visit. The care I could not give her and numerous little things she got to look forward to from you (1961).

- During my mother's last distressing months, Miss Dickert (my maiden name) was a source of great comfort and kind understanding and brought a noticeable joy to her at a time when there was little joy to be had. The effect of her calm efficiency and her cheerful manner should, I believe, be commended, and that is the purpose of this little note (1963).

- Mother wanted me to send you a note that her irises are at the nicest right now and if you'd like to see them she would be happy for you to stop if you happened to be in the neighborhood (1967). I did stop to see the iris!

- Thank you for the excellent care that you gave Helen during her illness. You helped make her problems more bearable, and she always looked forward to your visits (1967).

One reason that I share these personal letters from my "memory book" as a staff nurse is to note that patients and families did not dwell on my professional skills and competence as a nurse. This was, and is, an expectation! Comments referenced the personal, caring aspect of the care process that were and continue to be important to me as a nurse. I encourage every nurse to begin a memory book so that he or she can reflect on the letters and comments in the future and be reminded of the important role they had in the lives of many individuals.

During my 22 years as an administrator nursing provided the opportunity and privilege to meet many challenges but also experience many benefits. I have experienced personal and professional satisfaction. My commitment to professional nursing and quality patient care were and are important to me. I sought to provide a quality work environment for the staff, contractors and volunteers. This commitment to professional nursing resulted in personal and professional satisfaction, the opportunity to publish articles and books, state and national recognition, and the lifetime honor of membership in what I consider to be a rewarding and respected profession.

One unexpected, special benefit of my career as a home care nurse was that I met my husband, Charlie. In the early 1960s, both of us ate lunch on a regular basis at the same restaurant in the town where we both worked and later lived for almost 40 years. We married in 1969 and celebrated our 45th wedding anniversary on February 8, 2014. Charlie died September 12, 2014. God blessed us during our 45 year journey together.

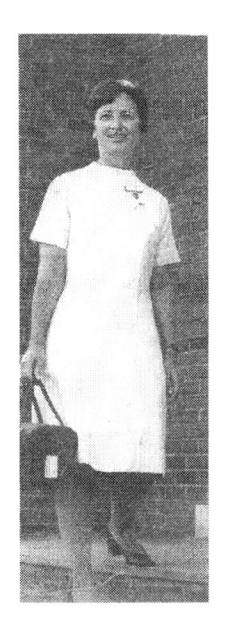

Student Nurse 1954-1957   Staff Visiting Nurse 1960-1972

Miss Dickert was Marilyn's name before 1969

Dear Nerssi?
I Like you.
You help pepile.
god Love you becalse
you help pepile.

You Tell on Yourself

You tell on yourself by the friends you seek,
By the very manner in which you speak,
By the way you employ your leisure time,
By the use you make of dollar and dime.

You tell what you are by the things you wear,
By the spirit in which your burdens bear,
By the kind of things at which you laugh,
By the records you play on the phonograph.

You tell what you are by the way you walk,
By the things of which you delight to talk,
By the manner in which you bear defeat,
By so simple a thing as how you eat.

By the book you choose from the well-filled shelves,
In these ways and more you tell on yourself,
So there's really no particle of sense,
In an effort to keep up false pretense.

This poem, by an unidentified author, is written in the front of the Scofield Reference Bible I received from my parents, Roger and Florence Dickert, for high school graduation on June 9, 1954. I was blessed with Christian parents and Sunday school teachers who were excellent role models during my first 18 years. I was taught to store God's word in my heart (Psalm 119:11. TLB) by reading the Bible and memorizing Bible verses. When I enrolled in Abington Memorial Hospital School of Nursing I moved away from home and was on my own for the first time. I often read the words of this poem that remind me that whatever I do as a person and professional reflects on my character.

Journeys Through All Seasons of Life

Ecclesiastes 3:1-2. *For everything there is a season, and a time for every matter under heaven: a time to be born and a time to die…*

The book: *"The Fall of Freddy the Leaf: A Story of Life for All Ages"* by Leo Buscaglia is one of my favorite books by a favorite author.

Freddy is a leaf. His friends are also leaves named, Alfred, Ben, Clare, and Daniel. Daniel is his best friend who explains many things to Freddy such as although all the leaves are from the same tree, all are different. Daniel also explains the purpose for each leaf: provide shade in the summer, to turn beautiful colors in the fall, to just do their job, and then they will die and fall gently to the ground. Daniel continues his explanation that the tree does not die, it has Life. Freddy experienced spring, summer, fall, and when winter came, Freddy's friends began to fall from the tree. Finally, Freddy fell from his branch and floated gently and softly to the ground. He had been a part of life, it made him proud and he was more comfortable than he had ever been.

Leo Buscaglia wrote this book for children who have suffered a permanent loss but I appreciate his message since it speaks of the seasons of my life. Ecclesiastes 3:1-2. For everything there is a season, and a time for every matter under heaven: a time to be born, and a time to die….

The book includes the contents of a note found in Leo Buscaglia's typewriter the day after his death on June 12, 1998. The note read: "Every moment spent in unhappiness is a moment of happiness lost." This note reminds me that I have 1440 moments/minutes each day to count my blessings and thank God for his love and care in each season of my life.

King Solomon said, "Have two goals: wisdom – that is, knowing and doing right – and common sense. Don't let them slip away, for they will fill you with living energy, and bring you honor and respect. They keep you safe from defeat and disaster and from stumbling off the trail. With them on guard you can sleep without fear; you need not be afraid of disaster or the plots of wicked men, for the Lord is with you; he protects you." (Proverbs 3:21-23 TLB).

My personal and professional experiences and relationships have been wonderful. They have spanned the seasons of life of my family, friends and patients. There have been detours along the path but I have been safe and not stumbled off the trail because of God's protection. I am thankful for my past journeys and look forward to the future journeys wherever they may take me. My prayer for everyone who shares my journeys is in the words of the song: "Make Me a Blessing to Someone Today".

I am honored to share my faith and some of my experiences with you through the devotions and reflections in *Journeys with God*. I invite you to share your journeys with me at mharris555@verizon.net.

Made in the USA
Middletown, DE
23 April 2016